Extreme
Rock & Ice
25 of the World's Great Climbs

NEW HOLLAND

Garth Hattingh

First published in 2000 by
New Holland Publishers
London • Cape Town • Sydney • Auckland

24 Nutford Place
London W1H 6DQ
United Kingdom

80 McKenzie Street
Cape Town 8001
South Africa

14 Aquatic Drive
Frenchs Forest, NSW 2086
Australia

218 Lake Road
Northcote, Auckland
New Zealand

ISBN 1 85974 513 X

Publisher Mariëlle Renssen
Managing Editors Claudia dos Santos (SA)
and Mari Roberts (UK)
Designer Mark Jubber
Design Assistant Geraldine Cupido
Editorial Assistance Elizé Lübbe, Leslie Brian
Cartographer John Loubser
Illustrator Steven Felmore
Picture Researcher Gill Gordon
Production Myrna Collins
Consultants Victor Saunders (UK) and
Greg Pritchard (Australia)

Reproduction by
Hirt & Carter (Pty) Ltd, Cape Town
Printed and bound in Singapore by
Craft (Pte) Ltd
2 4 6 8 10 9 7 5 3 1

Half title Superb ice on Sea of Vapours in Banff National Park, Canada, offers ice climbing at its very best.

Full title Steve Monks on the wet and wild initial pitch during the first free ascent of the Totem Pole in Tasmania.

Right Porters haul equipment on the last stretch to base camp near the remote Shipton Spire in the Karakorum.

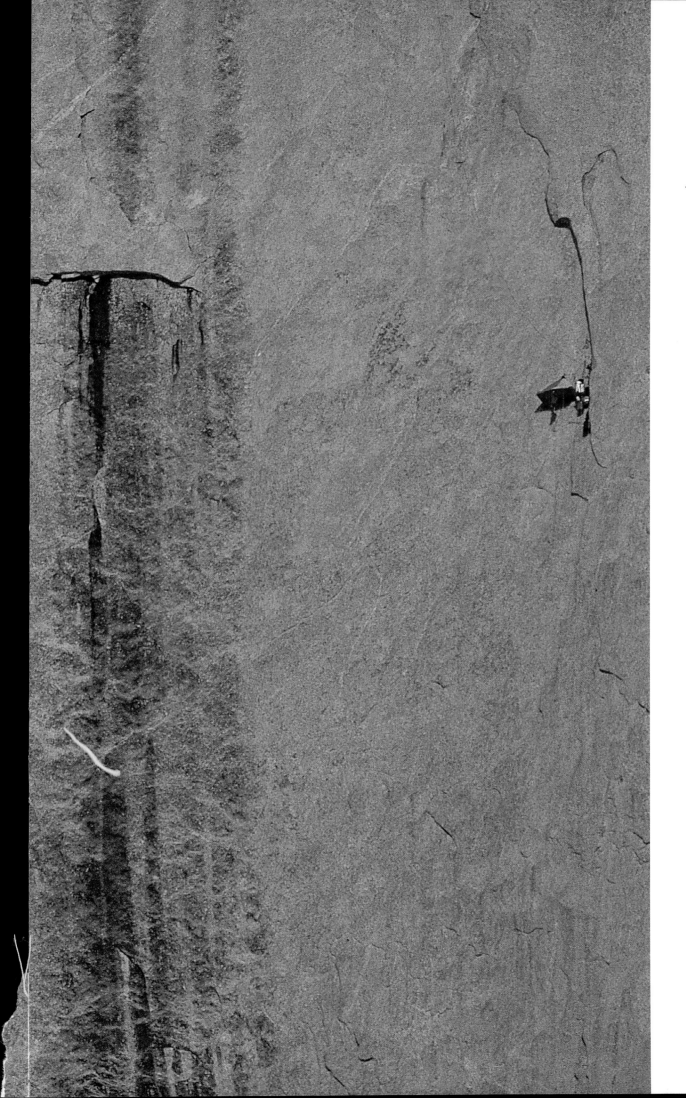

Foreword

AFTER MY ACCIDENT ON THE TOTEM POLE the one question nonclimbers asked repeatedly was, 'Why did you do it? Why did you nearly kill yourself just to climb a rock?'

Because it's there? Nonsense! For the adrenaline rush? That seems to be stated as a popular reason, yet I don't agree. You will experience an adrenaline rush every time you BASE jump or sky dive, but not when you're climbing, not even when you take climbing to its extreme. The answer to the question 'Why?' is much more complex than just a charge of chemicals to the brain.

The only activity I have found that comes close is yoga. The suppleness required to hold a position for several minutes, while the muscles scream as lactic acid floods in and the nerves stretch and become taut as steel cables – this is what resembles the extreme-climbing experience.

The mental agility and strength required to overcome the fear one feels while climbing is that of a master yogi. You live for one moment at a time, and when that moment is gone, there is the next one to contend with. To climb extreme routes an individual must transcend a conscious mind that is normally cluttered with menial day-to-day concerns, and focus on a different horizon.

The climbs in this book are about pain and dread. Whether it be the lung-bursting agony of a high-altitude climb in the Himalayas or the fear factor of soloing a big wall, these routes are enjoyed only in retrospect. When you are safely back, then, and only then, can you appreciate the magnificence of Great Trango's rock architecture or the beauty of an alpine sunrise.

Yoga teaches one not to look to an end but to appreciate the journey. This doctrine is applicable for climbing as well, and especially for extreme climbing. And what a journey it is!

PAUL PRITCHARD

Contents

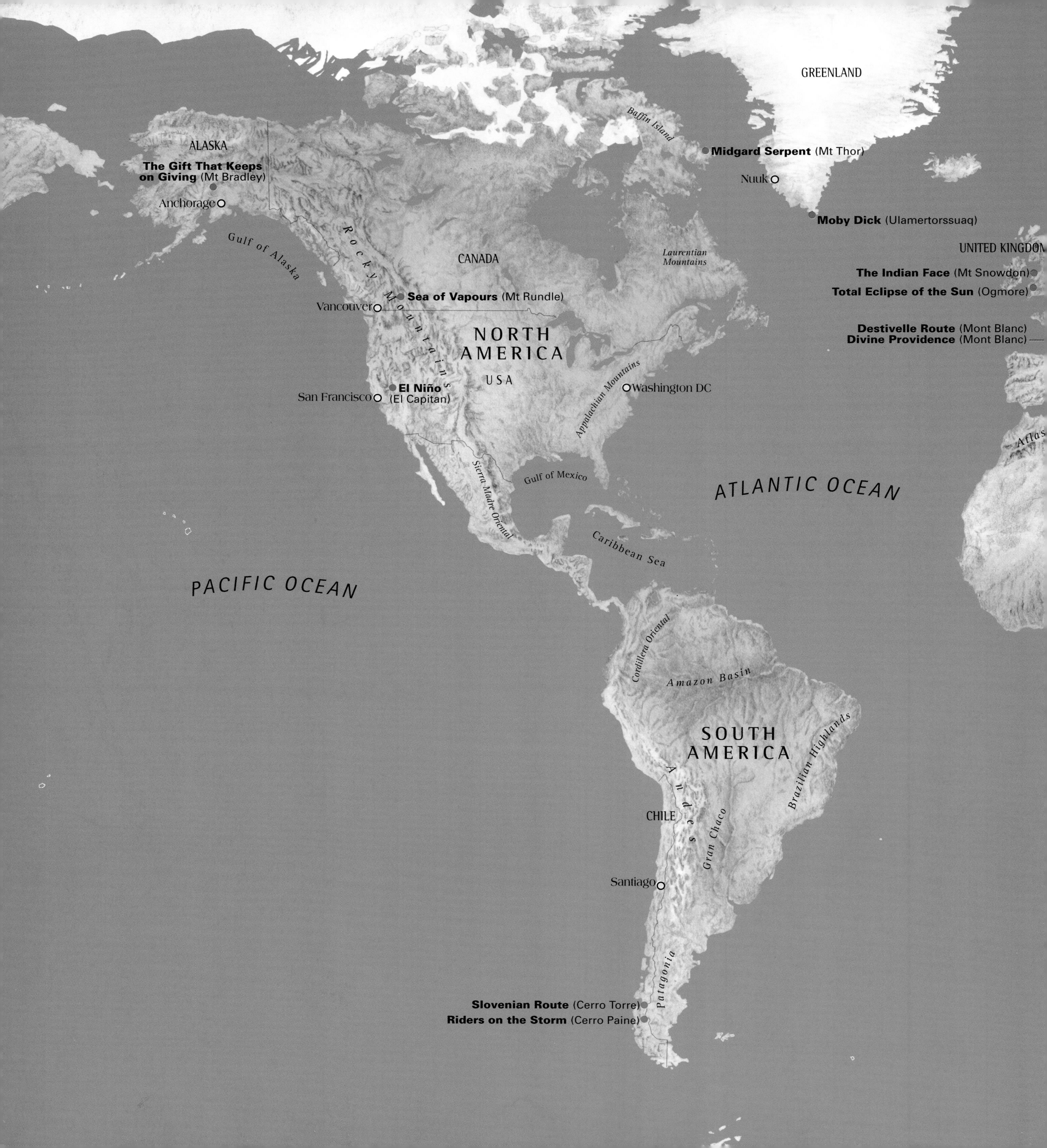

GREENLAND

Baffin Island

ALASKA

The Gift That Keeps
on Giving (Mt Bradley)

Anchorage O

● **Midgard Serpent** (Mt Thor)

Nuuk O

● **Moby Dick** (Ulamertorssuaq)

Gulf of Alaska

R o c k y   M o u n t a i n s

CANADA

Laurentian
Mountains

UNITED KINGDOM

The Indian Face (Mt Snowdon)
Total Eclipse of the Sun (Ogmore) ●

Sea of Vapours (Mt Rundle)

Vancouver O

NORTH
AMERICA

Destivelle Route (Mont Blanc)
Divine Providence (Mont Blanc)

USA

El Niño
(El Capitan)

San Francisco O

O Washington DC

Atlas

Sierra Madre Oriental

Gulf of Mexico

ATLANTIC OCEAN

Caribbean Sea

PACIFIC OCEAN

Cordillera Oriental

Amazon Basin

Brazilian Highlands

SOUTH
AMERICA

A
n
d
e
s

CHILE

Gran Chaco

Santiago O

Patagonia

Slovenian Route (Cerro Torre) ●
Riders on the Storm (Cerro Paine) ●

EUROPE
London
Great White Fright (Dover Cliffs)
Paris
Metanoia (Eiger)
FRANCE SWITZERLAND
Weg durch den Fisch (Mt Marmolada)
ITALY
Rome
The X-Files (Gran Paradiso)
The Empire Strikes Back (Gran Paradiso)

Mountains Mediterranean Sea

Sahara Desert

AFRICA

Ethiopian Highlands

Congo Basin

Great Rift Valley

Kalahari Basin

Drakensberg

Cape Town

Ural Mountains

Siberian Plateau

Zapadno Sibirskaya Ravina

Verkhoyanskiy Khrebet

ASIA

Golden Pillar (Spantik)
Grand Voyage (Great Trango Tower)
Hateja (Mt Beatrice)
Polish Route (K2)
Ship of Fools (Shipton Spire)

Plateau of Tibet

Himalayas

Lahore
PAKISTAN
Delhi
Lightning Route (Changabang)
South Face (Lhotse)
West Face (Gaurishankar)
NEPAL

Karachi

INDIA

Mumbai

PACIFIC OCEAN

INDIAN OCEAN

AUSTRALIA

Great Dividing Range

Adelaide
Sydney
Serpentine
(Mt Arapiles)
Melbourne

Hobart
Totem Pole (Cape Huay)

Introduction

'The hardest and most dangerous climb I have ever done'

Will Gadd talking about The Empire Strikes Back

THE URGE TO EXPLORE, TO PUSH THE LIMITS of the possible, appears to be an inbuilt trait in humankind. For many it remains hidden, never to emerge; for others, it becomes a way of life. Possibly this behaviour dates back to our cave-dwelling days when the surge of adrenaline accompanied the frequent hunts, or perhaps it is part of a nobler, more refined aspect of the human spirit.

For those who feature in this book – the extreme climbers – it is safe to say that the adventurous urge has come to dominate their being. The feats of endurance, determination and courage which have led to the successful (not to forget the even more frequent, unsuccessful) ascents of the climbs described here could not have come from casual, occasional climbers. Not all were (or are) fulltime, professional climbers – far from it; most practised climbing as a pastime or sport, often an all-consuming one.

The key features linking all of the climbers are dedication, boldness, commitment, and, some may argue, a touch of lunacy.

The selection of climbs in this book reflect the cutting edge of the sport over the past quarter-century, running right up to the end of the millennium. An attempt has been made to cover the various disciplines into which modern climbing has evolved, including the most risky of rock, ice, big-wall and high-mountain routes.

Each generation of climbers has sought to define their own goals, to stamp their own pattern on the fabric of mountaineering. Trends have emerged to counteract the way in which advances in equipment and techniques, transport and facilities have tamed some of the extreme efforts of previous generations.

The first 75 years of the 20th century

The first 25 years followed hard on the heels of the so-called Golden Age of climbing, during which virtually all the peaks of greater Europe had seen first (and often, many repeated) ascents. What was left was to do harder, more daring routes on these peaks, and explore the further ranges of the world. This was largely put on hold by the wars that marked the turn of the century, with the most devastating of these, World War I, putting paid to many a climber's aspirations (and the lives of some great climbers). Immediately after this war, eyes turned to the Himalayas, and reconnaissance climbs were staged to the 8000m (26,000ft) peaks. None of these was to succeed (although doubt still exists over George Mallory and Andrew Irvine's 1924 Everest attempt).

The years from 1925 to 1950 saw the great ranges being fairly quiet, probably as a result of a combination of political instability and economics. Tremendously bold climbs were, however, done in Europe, with most of the great Alpine faces being climbed, culminating in the ascent of the North Face of the Eiger in 1938, the eve of World War II. The war put a halt to further climbing, and when it ended, climbing resumed slowly and tentatively, with few significant ascents in Europe, although the USA saw a good deal of activity, particularly in Colorado.

Foreword John Middendorf and Xavier Bongard adrift in a sea of granite on Grand Voyage, Great Trango Tower.

Contents Ascending fixed ropes high above the K2 glacier on the North Ridge of K2 in the expedition of 1996.

Previous pages A climber's temporary home dangles from the rock on the vastness of El Capitan in the Yosemite Valley.

Opposite, left to right Three differing camps: base camp on the moraine just below Shipton Spire; base camp in the valley beneath the Great Trango Tower; a somewhat more elevated site on the Nameless Tower, in the Trango group.

Right British climber Steve Sustad is dwarfed by Jannu, in the Himalayas of eastern Nepal.

The world and climbers needed a victory to heal the wounds of the war, and the ascent of Annapurna in 1950 and then Everest in 1953 provided just that. Suddenly climbing was news, was bold and heroic. A spate of attempts and successes on peaks in the Himalayas followed, with all 14 of the 8000m (26,000ft) main summits achieved by 1964. In the Americas, Mt Robson and Mt McKinley saw renewed activity, and climbers started to stream to all corners of the globe in search of virgin summits. The second Golden Age had begun. As an offshoot of the large mountain activity, there was a huge growth in pure rock climbing, and the USA, UK, Europe and many other areas saw the opening of large numbers of routes of steadily increasing difficulty.

The last quarter-century

By 1975 most of the notable large peaks had been climbed by at least one route, and roads and railways had been pushed into regions which previously had been difficult to access. Climbs and peaks which had been the domain of only the most hardy fanatics became populated with scores of weekend climbers, many being guided up routes which only a decade or so before had been the realm of the pioneers. Even climbs such as the 1953 'desperate route' up Everest has now become a virtual tourist trail (although frighteningly dangerous, considering the 1996 disaster season when six climbers died).

In search of their own challenges, climbers started to explore new avenues. The bold three-day lightweight dash up and down the northwest face of the 8068m (26,470ft) Gasherbrum I (Hidden Peak) by Reinhold Messner and Peter Habeler in 1975 forced climbers to rethink styles of ascent on even the 8000m (26,000ft) giants. The concept of 'alpine-style' climbs on peaks which had largely been the realm of large, cumbersome expeditionary-style climbing brought about a spate of bold attempts by small groups, and paved the way for solo ascents of these giants. The Pole Wojtek Kurtyka and England's Alex McKintyre repeated this sort of audacious attempt with their route up the northeast face of Dhaulagiri (8167m; 26,795ft) in 1980. Kurtyka later teamed up with his countryman, Jerzy Kukuczka in perhaps even more daring routes on Broad Peak (8047m; 26,402ft), Gasherbrum II (8167m; 26,795ft) and Gasherbrum I in 1983. Many others pioneered difficult routes via the 'one-single-committed-push' philosophy. Oxygenless attempts on the higher of the 8000m (26,000ft) peaks were heralded by Messner and Habeler's success on Mt Everest in 1978. Then came Messner's solo new-route ascent of Everest in 1980, which set a new challenge. Messner also holds the distinction of being the first person to ascend all 14 of the 8000m (26,000ft) peaks – a goal many climbers still aspire to.

At the same time, the great granite walls of the Yosemite Valley were producing another form of climbing, one that sought to eliminate the many days of bivouacking needed to complete the long aid routes that were the feature of valley climbs. The big push towards free-climbing the routes had begun, which is being continued to its logical conclusion by the current speed attempts. The techniques (and equipment) forged in the valley were soon to spread across the globe, opening the way for climbers to succeed on desperate big wall climbs in Patagonia, the Karakorum, Canada, Alaska, and more recently, Greenland and Baffin Island.

1979	1981	1983	1984	1986	1986
West Face	The Fish	Great White Fright	Divine Providence	The Indian Face	Polish Route
Gaurishankar	Marmolada	Dover cliffs	Mont Blanc	Mt Snowdon	K2
East Nepalese Himalayas	Italy	England	Italy	Wales	Pakistani Karakorum
Big Mountain	*Alpine scale*	*Ice & Mixed*	*Alpine scale*	*Rock*	*Big Mountain*

The traditional rock climbers were not quiet either. British, Australian and American climbers in particular started to seek out harder (frequently riskier) routes. At the cutting edge of the sport, the points of protection for the leader became fewer and less secure, the lead-outs longer, the angles steeper. Solo climbing of long, multipitch climbs became more frequent, and climbing started to become news, unfortunately also gaining a reputation for being dangerous (which was in many cases an undeniable fact and, in the perverse way of humankind, served to act as an incentive to many). Training for climbing in a professional way crept in, and climbing grades rose steadily.

On other fronts, the trends in climbing were changing in a direction which many climbers found disquieting – the advent of bolt-protected sport climbs. The movement gained impetus in France, where in many areas soft limestone cliffs were eminently climbable, but lacked safe protection for the lead climber. The highly gymnastic form of climbing which developed, where falls are non-serious and have become an acceptable part of the game, appeals to many, and the trend soon spread across the globe. Today there are thousands of sport routes on all types of rock, and the hardest grades demand intense dedication, commitment and physical strength. Many of the highly gymnastic skills pioneered in sport climbing are now being used in other forms of climbing.

A field that saw rapid growth was that of ice climbing in its own right. Snow and ice had always been an accepted part of getting up alpine and big mountain routes in Europe, Asia and elsewhere. Scotland, in particular, had developed a reputation as the hard ice centre of the world, with its precarious mixed (a combination of ice and rock) winter routes on Ben Nevis, Ben McDhui and other crags. It was, however, only in the mid-1970s that ice climbing really began to catch the attention of climbers, first in the USA and Europe, and eventually the rest of the world. The opening of Polar Circus in the Canadian Rockies (700m/2296ft of hard, waterfall ice) in 1975 brought the activity into the limelight, and soon radical designs of ice axes and crampons appeared in climbing shops. The magnificent waterfall ice of Vail, in Colorado, and the Canadian Rockies in general, as well as many parts of Europe and Asia, started to receive visits from rock climbers who had now found something they could do in the cold winter months. As equipment improved and the number of pure virgin ice waterfalls started to diminish, so the concept of mixed climbing hit the world (Scottish climbers would argue that it was nothing new to them), and routes of frightening nature began to appear, such as the Sea of Vapours, on page 63–65.

The equipment revolution

The range and quality of equipment available to the climber was also in the process of evolution. Advances in technology produced 'miracle fibres' as well as composite rubbers and plastics, such as polyfibre, Goretex, polyamides, Teflon, Kevlar, and carbon-fibre, which affected the design of ropes, inner and outer garments, shoes, slings and even handles of axes. Lighter, warmer, more robust, water- and windproof, stickier, stronger – all of these aided and abetted the extreme mountaineer's armoury. Space-age (literally!) metal compounds, with lightweight aluminum strengthened with titanium, beryllium, and a host of other elements led

1987	1988	1990	1990	1991	1991
Golden Pillar	Serpentine	South Face	Riders on the Storm	Metanoia	Destivelle Route
Spantik	The Grampians	Lhotse	Central Tower of Paine	Eiger	Petit Dru
Hispar Karakorum	Australia	East Nepalese Himalayas	Chile, Patagonia	Switzerland	France
Big Mountain	*Rock*	*Big Mountain*	*Big Wall*	*Ice & Mixed*	*Alpine scale*

to virtually unbreakable crampon and axe points, to featherweight carabiners, and to hi-tech nuts and camming devices. Battery drills powerful enough to drill into hard rock and epoxy resins stronger than steel gave climbers the weapons needed to establish lines of bolts on any rock face they desired.

Mallory and Irvine would have been hard-pressed to recognize the modern, brightly coloured Goretex- and fleece-swaddled climbers with their body-contouring rucksacks, lightweight oxygen bottles, plastic boots and other modern trimmings as being of their species. In the same way, Edward Whymper, the renowned 19th-century climber, and his compatriots would gaze in wonder at the modern, cheerfully plumaged alpinist, bedecked with carabiners, nuts, 'friends', and other iron-mongery, and connected by a thin web of brightly patterned nylon ropes.

The obvious question is whether all this equip-ment made climbing any easier. The answer is yes. There is no doubt that the climber on the standard routes of the Matterhorn or Everest has an easier time than the first ascensionists, and modern equipment plays no small role in this.

Has it made climbing any less dangerous? The answer once again is yes – but this time, with an added caution. By and large, equipment advances should, and have, made climbing a safer sport. However, as recent tragedies have shown, climbers have no guarantee of safety, particularly on the higher peaks. Weather, avalanches, rockfalls, and above all, human error, infuse climbing with the risk element that is so much part of its nature. This applies as much to the soloist on a sea cliff who disregards the tide, or the climber on a sport route who ties on incorrectly, as it does to the guided climber on K2.

In the final analysis, climbing involves risk. And this is the spice of the game – many top climbers would abandon their sport if there were no risk involved. The extreme climber is one who ensures that the odds are not 100 percent in his or her favour, who chooses the climb or the route which will not give guaranteed safety, and guar-anteed success. If the standard route up a peak has been tamed, then do it in winter, do it solo, eliminate any points of aid, or find a new and much more difficult pathway, a smaller but yet-

unclimbed peak with an impossible-looking line on it. The realm of the extreme climber is the realm of the just-possible-if-things-go-well.

The new millennium

Now that we have entered the new millennium, one might well ask, 'What next?' What challenges are the climbers of the new generation going to discover, what are their goals going to be? Is there any real adventure left for climbers?

Once again, the answer is yes – this time, a resounding one. In his introduction to *World Mountaineering,* the legendary Chris Bonington describes a valley in Tibet he visited in 1997 which is 'as extensive as the whole of Switzerland with over 20 magnificent jagged peaks in the 6000m (19,500ft) range, none of which have ever been attempted'.

There are still many regions of the world for mountaineers to explore; countless new variations or new routes on rock faces and big walls; many climbs to be repeated in winter, or solo, or climbed in 'better style' or 'faster' than they have been. Link-ups of a number of peaks, ski descents, night

1993	1994	1995	1997	1997	1998	1998
Sea of Vapours	Moby Dick	Totem Pole	Ship of Fools	X-Files	El Niño	Lightning Route
Mt Rundle	Ulamertorssuaq	Cape Huay	Shipton Spire	Val Valeile	El Capitan	Changabang
Canada	Greenland	Tasmania	Pakistani Karakorum	Italy	USA	Garwhal Himalayas
Ice & Mixed	*Big Wall*	*Rock*	*Big Wall*	*Ice & Mixed*	*Big Wall*	*Big Mountain*

The games extreme climbers play

climbs, a reversion to nonintrusive aid climbing with technology yet to be developed – who can predict what will be? The 'new era' regions such as Baffin Island, Greenland, newly accessible parts of China, South America and Alaska will undoubtedly see significant developments. A safe bet is that climbers, being the sort of people they are, will seek out these and other challenges, and adjust the odds such that there will always be new extreme climbs, and new extreme climbers. If one could have three wishes, they are that:

▲ These modern gladiators will recognize the finite nature of the earth, and tailor their actions so as to preserve climbs and climbing areas in as pristine a form as possible.

▲ With the vast range of modern climbing devices and techniques available, one would hope that they will have the humility to be subdued by the route, rather than to subdue it by totally artificial means, thus leaving some challenges for the succeeding generation.

▲ They will have fun, share adventures, and return home to tell their tales to future generations. To future extreme climbers – go well, and 'Berg Heil!'

In the climbing world, one of the most influential short essays has been that of American author Lito Tejeda Flores, who wrote an article entitled 'Games Climbers Play' (published in a volume of stories and essays entitled *Games Climbers Play*). Flores' premise was simple; his expansion on it was profound (and also very humorous).

The premise was that climbing is a game, and as such is played by rules. The expansion indicated that, unlike most games, climbers change the rules to suit the circumstances, to level the playing field, and, strangely enough, to stack the odds such that the mountain has a chance of winning.

Herein lies the unique nature of the climbing game. If the rules of engagement are too easy, and victory is ensured, then the (true?) climber alters the parameters, making it more difficult to succeed and making the whole exercise more risky. There are certainly cases where this subterfuge is not needed – any ascent of K2, Everest or, for that matter, the Salathé Wall or Moose's Tooth (to name a few examples; there are many more in this book) is a risk. But, as previously discussed, modern equip-

ment may make the standard route too easy, thus a new route is selected to create a suitably challenging 'game'. The extreme climber may scorn the normal route up K2, going instead for a new, untried variant, or decide to climb it solo, without oxygen, in less than 24 hours. If a rock climb has been done with points of aid, the challenge is to climb it 'free' ('The North Face of the Eiger has been done by a lot of folk in summer? Fine, let us do it in winter'). Sometimes, a whole new game plan is invented to raise the odds, such as capsule-style ascents and mixed climbing.

Here are a few of the games that extreme climbers play: some of them will appear in their 'pure' form in this book, others will surface as parts of a greater whole. Often extreme climbing involves a mixture of these discrete games to achieve success, and the overlap or synthesis of these may constitute no small part of the extreme nature of the climb. Each is neither a greater nor a lesser form of the sport, merely different, much as a 100m dash and a 10,000m race defy direct comparison, both demanding absolute commitment at the top levels of athletic performance.

1998	1998	1998	1998	1999	1999	2000
Grand Voyage	Midgard Serpent	Hateja	Slovenian Route	The Gift	Total Eclipse	Empire Strikes Back
Great Trango Tower	Mt Thor	Beatrice	Cerro Torre	Mt Bradley	Ogmore	Val Valeile
Balto Karakorum	Baffin Island	Pakistani Karakorum	Argentina, Patagonia	Alaska	Wales	Italy
Big Wall	*Big Wall*	*Big Mountain*	*Big Wall*	*Alpine scale*	*Rock*	*Ice & Mixed*

Rock Climbs

Totem Pole. Serpentine. The Indian Face. Total Eclipse.

THE URGE TO CLIMB SEEMS TO BE INBORN – toddlers climb up furniture, and as they grow older – trees, poles, and roofs. Rock climbing is a natural extension of mankind's instinctive tendency to explore his surroundings.

Rock climbing as a sport is only a century or so old, beginning with the tradition of the wealthy gentry 'rambling in the countryside', which led naturally to scrambling up rock, and then serious climbing with ropes, slings and other paraphernalia. The European Alps became the playground of the first adventurous characters, and the occupation of guiding clients came into being. Slowly the sport spread to include all levels of society, ceasing to be exclusively the domain of the idle rich. Local crags replaced the Alps, and climbing for fun on any suitable piece of rock became as popular as climbing a mountain peak to its summit.

Rock climbing is at the core of all climbing – the equipment and techniques are shared by the sport expert, the deep-water soloist, the ice climber, the alpinist, the big-wall climber and high-altitude expert. Some common elements include balance, strength, protection (equipment placed or fastened into the rock or ice to hold the climber in case of a fall, while on a ledge or at a belay point), use of the rope for belaying (safeguarding the other climber with the rope) and good judgement. There are millions of rock climbers, whose activities range from bouldering (climbing on small outcrops without using gear) to sport climbing (climbing using bolts preplaced in the rock as protection points), and casual climbing on small crags to desperate climbs on walls hundreds of metres high.

The nature of extreme rock climbs is that they are serious – that is, the consequences of falling off are dire. In the climbs chosen for this book, Martin Crocker's deep-water solo at Ogmore certainly fits the bill, as beneath the seemingly safe waters lurk hidden rocks, and treacherous currents lie in wait for the fallen climber. Areas such as the Calanque in France, Dorset in the UK in summer, and portions of the Portuguese and Spanish coasts boast superb venues that are the deep-water soloist's dream.

The Totem Pole is no less serious; it is sparsely protected, and once again the climber is at the mercy of tide and current – just in reaching the climb via a dangerous abseil – with loose rock abounding. The committing nature of Serpentine and Indian Face are similarly unquestionable, with long lead-outs above marginal protection placements – in the words of Jerry Moffat, of Master's Wall fame, 'This is no place to mess up!'

Thus, although these climbs perhaps cannot compare in length or objective dangers – such as crevasses, avalanches and remoteness – with some of the longer routes in other sections of this book, they share the same extreme criteria: failure to complete a sequence of moves, inadequate preparation, poor planning or simply bad luck could lead to 'damage or death'. Rock climbs are given alpha-numerical grades (see p157) taking into account the physical effort needed, the nature of the rock, the amount and type of protection, and the technical quality of the climbing moves. It is no surprise that the climbs discussed are (or were at the time of their ascent) at the top of their respective grading systems.

Previous pages The power of the mind – Lynn Hill (USA) on the crux second pitch of Serpentine, Taipan Wall, Australia.
Opposite, left to right Steve Monks, hanging on tight, on the second pitch of The Free Route (25), Totem Pole, Tasmania; absolute concentration on an ultimate route – Andrew Dunbar tenuously snaking his way up Serpentine, the Grampians; Johnny Dawes on the extremely thin crux section during the first ascent of The Indian Face, Clogwyn Du'r Arddu, Wales.
Right Martin Crocker on the difficult exit cracks of Total Eclipse of the Sun, his epic deep-water solo at Ogmore, Wales.

Totem Pole – Cape Huay

Breaking a sea stack's spell

THE ISLAND OF TASMANIA, THE SMALLEST state in Australia, lies off the southeastern corner of the continent. Until 1856, it was known as Van Diemen's Land, and was initially a highly unpopular destination, serving as a penal colony for Australian and British miscreants. It now goes by the name of the Holiday Isle, still importing many people per year, but this time as visitors – tourism being one of its major income sources. The island offers tremendously varied scenery, and good skiing in the eastern highlands during the winter months.

For most climbers, the mountains at about 1600m (5250ft) are not really spectacular enough to be considered alpine climbing, but the numerous small cliffs are still good for cragging, and the 3200km (2000 miles) of indented coastline has some of the finest sea-cliff climbing in the world. There are a large number of small islands, and numerous dramatic sea stacks.

Not far from the capital city, Hobart, is the Tasman Peninsula, which projects southward into the icy waters of the aptly named Storm Bay (more properly known as Maingon Bay).

On the most easterly point of the Fortesque Peninsula (a sort of sub-branch of the Tasman Peninsula) is Cape Huay, which terminates in a number of sea stacks running northeast. Between Cape Huay and Mitre Rock, a 120m (400ft) mini-island, are two truly amazing projections, the Candlestick and the Totem Pole.

The sea stacks

From most angles, the 65m (215ft) Totem Pole tends to be overshadowed by its more visible neighbour, the Candlestick. The latter is about 100m (330ft) high, and roughly 25m (80ft) in cross-section at its base. Its tremendous height versus small girth makes it resemble a large candlestick, although many people may see more phallic similarities! It has been climbed by a number of routes – most relatively easy but still dangerous because of large numbers of enormous, loose blocks.

The smaller Totem Pole, when eventually seen in profile, acts as a magnet to climbers. The 65m-high (215ft) dolerite pillar rises straight out of the cold, deep blue water, lofting almost magically to a detached-looking top block. The base section is no more than 8m (25ft), making it a needle to be reckoned with indeed. From a short distance, it appears to be an unbroken monolithic spire; closer examination reveals a few horizontal faults and the odd thin vertical crack.

The route

The remote and isolated Totem Pole is approached on foot – a two-and-a-half-hour walk on the Cape Huay Trail through the low sea-cliff bush to the top of the mainland peninsula. This is where the interesting bit starts – a 90m (300ft) abseil down the broken and dangerous dolerite of the mainland onto a tiny shelf just above (mean) water level.

Route
Totem Pole, free route

Grade
Grade 25

Area
Cape Huay, Tasmania

Length
70m (230ft), due to winding route

Date of first ascent
1995

Climbers
Steve Monks, Simon Mentz, Jane Wilkinson, Simon Carter (all of Australia)

Opposite Australian Roxanne Wells on the first female-lead ascent of the needle-like Totem Pole Free Route (Grade 25) – her ascent was made into a nail-biting television short that is well worth watching.

The swell running from the northern end of Fortesque Bay to the Munro Bight in the south can get rather large without too much warning, and there is no guarantee that the climbers will still be dry at the end of the abseil.

It is worth mentioning that it was at this point that the well-known British climber, Paul Pritchard, had his near-fatal accident when a shoebox-sized block was dislodged, landing on him and causing serious paralysis. He was eventually lifted out in a dramatic and highly technical rescue.

From the small sea-platform it is a bold (and also cold and wet) few metres that has to be negotiated on seaweed-slippery rock that only just protrudes from the water at the bottom point of the swell at low tide. This enables climbers to scramble up a metre or so onto a spray-battered ledge on the pillar.

The original, and to date only, complete route on the Totem Pole itself is interesting – it spirals virtually right around the pillar, starting from the western corner, closest to the mainland, and then running anti-clockwise to the small ledge below the final few metres of pinnacle.

The climbers

Steve Monks has been active on the Australian scene for a few decades, putting up scary traditional routes and mega-desperate sport routes alike. He is a prolific new-router, who has spied out and opened a number of excellent crags, including the Fortress (South Grampians) areas of Mt Stapylton and a number of the Tasman Peninsula's best.

Simon Mentz started climbing in 1988, and has been incredibly active since then. He has also added a number of significant new routes to the Australian scene, particularly in the Grampians. Compatriot Jane Wilkinson is an experienced and very accomplished climber, and she has seconded Steve on a number of his major routes.

Opposite American Lynn Hill, crossing spray-laden, slippery rock, braves the swell on the second ascent of the The Variant to the Free Route (Grade 24).
Right Steve Monks, belayed by a soggy Jane Wilkinson on the first pitch, first ascent. The original route moves up and right where The Variant moves left. Falling off before the first protection is not a good idea!

Simon Carter is recognized not only as a good climber, but also as one of the leading climbing photographers in the world, and Australia's finest. He has been documenting the recent history of Australian climbing on film for a number of years now, and has written two books exclusively on climbing in Australia.

The climb

A number of climbers had eyed the Totem Pole for a considerable time, and eventually Steve Monks, persuaded by Simon Mentz, decided that it was too good an opportunity to miss. They invited Jane Wilkinson, and then threw in Australia's best

climbing photographer, Simon Carter, to make sure that the climb was recorded in fine style.

Preliminary investigation was made on abseil, and a likely looking direct line (which eventually turned out to be impractical) was spotted. At first light the group made their way along the trail to the top of Cape Huay, and set up the two-stage abseil. The top of the lower stage would be the key to the

way off, via a Tyrolean traverse. Eventually the three climbers were perched on the tiny wave-cut base platform, already getting soaked from the spray. It needed no invitation for Steve to move across to the base of the Totem Pole, experiencing a healthy dose of cold feet in the process! Simon Mentz and Jane followed, while the photographer initially kept dry taking the shots from the mainland.

Above An awesome view down the dolerite stack to Steve Monks and Jane Wilkinson at the top of the first pitch. The belay stance appears to be almost purpose-built, safely out of reach of the deceptively calm-looking sea below.

Opposite The moment of truth – Tyrolean traversing off the pillar is both exhilarating and nerve-wracking. A seemingly relaxed Nancy Feagin, from Australia, shows how it should be done.

Steve set off on the lead, and immediately realized that this was not going to be a simple climb. The rock at the base is both smooth and damp, and singularly unprotected for a good few metres. He was soon forced to traverse diagonally rightwards, using the corner for a partial lay-away, feet smearing on wet, slippery rock until thankfully a crack was found on the face that would take both hands and protection. By the time he reached the top of the crack, and a tiny belay block on the seaward side of the pillar, the belayers below were both soaked from the high swells and the spray. They moved up to join him as fast as their cold hands would let them.

The second pitch proved no easier than the first – the rock continued to offer few handholds, and after a series of desperate smearing moves, the leader (Simon Mentz) was forced to rely on marginal friction holds on the fairly round-edged corner to inch upwards, moving slowly higher and higher above any worthwhile protection. The spiralling continued, with Simon being compelled to shift right around the pillar into a thin vertical finger crack facing the open sea. Slowly but surely he led up this delicate, nerve-wracking section until he reached the large sloping ledge below the final block. The rest were quick to join him, and all that remained was to cross fingers and hope that the top block was more stable than it looked. A relatively easy crack led to the top of the 5m (16ft) block forming the head of the Totem Pole; the only way down was of course to down-climb this.

The party climbed with the bottom end of their abseil rope tied to the second climber, thereby giving a rope across to the mainland. Some firm points on the top block were established, the rope pulled tight, and Steve moved carefully out on the single thin line above the chasm below, dragging himself and another rope across to solid ground. The others tyroleaned across to join him, and then pulled the ropes. The Totem Pole had been bested, its spell was broken.

The climb has since been repeated a number of times, including a recent televised first female ascent, by the Australian climber, Roxanne Wells. The cameraman was none other than Steve Monks, with Simon Carter as stills photographer!

A noteworthy variant has been climbed by the well-known American, Lynn Hill.

Serpentine – Grampians

A sinuous line in the Great Outback

THE GRAMPIANS ARE A BUNCH OF RATHER wild and woolly mountains in the south of Victoria, Australia. Within the area of spiky bush and brightly coloured rock walls lie a good number of superb climbing areas, ranging from short sport climbs of any conceivable grade to longish traditionally protected routes.

Included in this range of mountains (although some climbers try to place it as a world apart) is the world-renowned Mt Arapiles, and the more recent wonder-cliff area, Mt Stapylton. Indeed, these two climbing venues hold some of the greatest Australian classic lines, such as the thin hand crack through an 8m (26ft) roof – Passport to Insanity (27) on The Fortress – and the new(ish) super-desperates such as You're Terminated (31) and Punks in the Gym (32) on Arapiles.

The rock in the area is immaculate hard sandstone, with a spectacular range of colours from the red-streaked grey walls of Mt Temple to the overhanging grey-streaked orange of the Taipan Wall.

The crag

Mt Stapylton, lying in the climbing shadow of the famous Arapiles, was fairly unexplored for a long time. The Taipan Wall was a grand discovery, and is regarded as the prime area on Mt Stapylton. It is 1.6km (1 mile) of mostly overhanging wall, averaging a height of 60m (200ft). The first major ascent of this wall happened in 1966, when

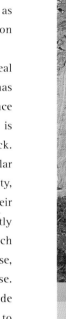

Michael Stone, accompanied by Ian Guild, climbed a diagonal meandering 110m (360ft) line up the wall, finishing on The Crag (or Central Tower).

This route was called The Seventh Pillar and is graded 5+/A4, making it (still) one of the hardest routes ever done in Victoria. It took two and a half days, and needed 17 bolts and a good number of pitons. The route overhangs by 23m (75ft)! Recent rebolting and regrading sees it as 18/M2, or Grade 23 or 28 free (depending on which variation is used).

Stapylton started to receive a great deal of attention in the mid-1980s, and has seen extensive development since then. To many, Australia is still the Great Outback. Australians, in particular the climbing fraternity, are notorious for their laid-back and slightly anarchistic approach to life, the Universe, and everything else. However, this attitude does not always extend to personal liberties taken with the rock, and some interesting controversies have arisen over bolts placed where natural gear is both possible and desirable.

Many of the Australian routes have an interesting approach to protection – where a camming device or a nut can be used, it is; where nothing but a bolt will do, a bolt is placed. On both sides of this (one might argue) sensible middle ground is the exception, where some climbers refuse to use any bolts at all and do wildly led-out routes which court death. Others argue that 'sport

Route	
Serpentine	
Grade	
Grade 31	
Area	
The Taipan Wall, Mt Stapylton, Grampians, Australia	
Length	
73m (240ft)	
Date of first ascent	
May 1988	
Climber	
Malcolm ('HB') Matheson (Australia)	

Opposite Gordon Poultney nearing the top on Serpentine, the *pièce de résistance* on the relentlessly overhanging Taipan Wall. The route is characterized by long lead-outs on marginal protection, and requires strenuous, powerful moves.

One such is Briton Andy Pollit's Sport Crack (26) cynically described as 'A fun little route with six bolts and a rap chain next to a perfect friend crack'. (*Mountain* 140)

The route

Serpentine starts some 60m (200ft) to the right of the Central Tower, on the upper Taipan Wall. It starts alarmingly straight up for a good few metres, then joins the Lawrence of Arabia traverse, scuttling quite a distance left until it finds itself below the highest point of the cliff. Here the line turns upwards again, to a belay point below a series of flakes. Rage (29) now joins it, then moves left around a bulging flake, while Serpentine moves off right. The line is now viciously over-hanging, and takes off in a sinuous fashion (guess where the name comes from), winding its way up the front of the Central Tower to emerge dead in the middle of the final crazily angled scoop that marks the cliff's zenith.

The climber

Malcolm ('HB') Matheson is a legend in Australian climbing. A frantically active climber, he has put up an unbelievable number of high-quality routes throughout the country, but in particular in the Grampians, and more recently on Taipan Wall. When protection problems reared their head, his attitude was, 'Solve it.' From this came a new breed of bolt (hexagonal, and slightly alarming at first), hanger (removable, with a small scallop in the top that allows it to hang straight on the bolt – climbers were stealing too many of the fixed variety!), tiny brass micro-wedges (called HBs – hence his nickname) which made protection possible in small cracks, and cams and rollers to solve the larger crack problems.

A notoriously wild driver, who revels in souped-up cars, parties and sheer fun, Matheson seems set to keep on going for many a year yet.

The climb

In 1987, Matheson had a go at the huge blank wall below the Central Tower, which most Australian climbers saw as the 'first great problem' of Taipan Wall (the 'last great problem', so they say, is up the glass-like overhanging blank wall left of Serpentine – which still awaits a line).

climbing is bolt climbing' and bolt the entire line. For many visiting sport climbers used to bolts, bolts and more bolts, the idea of 'semi-bolted' lines is anathema, and they refuse to climb these mixed-protection routes either on principle, or because they lack the skills to place trad gear. This is used as a justification for bolting routes that can be partially (or completely) protected on natural gear such as nuts, wires and cams. In some areas, this all-out bolting has been accepted; in others it still causes controversy; in some it is totally banned by the climbing fraternity. The Taipan Wall has not been excepted from these activities, and a few harsh words have been said about the practice of bolting alongside eminently pro-tectable (i.e. by traditional means) crack lines.

The lower section repulsed all attempts, and Matheson was forced to look further and further right for a starting point. Preliminary examination saw a line which he soon realized was going to take supreme fitness.

In 1988, Malcolm decided, 'That little piece of wall isn't going to beat me,' and started to train specifically for the route. Weight training put on the bulk he needed for the power moves he knew were coming on the upper crux pitch, and plenty of general climbing training made sure he was fully honed for the event. Eventually, a few months of extensive training later, he felt ready for the challenge, and set off on working the line.

The climb is a fine example of 'minimalist bolt protection', with every single piece that would go on natural gear being protected with wires and cams. The long, rising, leftwards traverse at Grade 24 turned out to be the crux for the belayer ('you can't ask for a tight rope on that piece!') but the 40m (130ft) pitch that followed was the one that needed the most preparation from HB. Taking fall after fall on minute and sometimes insecure wire nut placements, he slowly worked out the sequence needed to redpoint the pitch.

The mental and physical endurance that was needed to complete this climb – at the time probably the hardest in the Grampians and definitely one of the hardest in the world – should not be underestimated. Every fall was a setback, and added to the tension was the question, 'Will that piece of gear hold?'

For nine days he plugged away at the pitch, working out the minute shifts of body weight that would allow him to lay-back off the tiny flakes; getting to grips with the sloping handholds that relied on just the precise amount of friction, sorting out exactly how far he had to dyno to

Opposite American Lynn Hill shows her mastery on the intricate, energy-sapping start to the second pitch (Grade 29/ 5.13b/8a). A long lunge onto a tiny hold is needed to pass this overhang.
Below, left to right Lynn winds her way up the 40m (130ft) of the top pitch, allowing herself a much-needed 'rest' on the flake after the strenuous set of crux moves. Although the gear is preplaced, the climb is still at the limits of the possible.
Top right It is only when seen from the side that the overhanging nature of Serpentine becomes apparent.

latch onto a matchbox-sized hold. Eventually he was ready, and managed to fit the entire sequence together without a fall – the successful redpoint ascent of the hardest route in Australia was his.

The route drew climbers from all over the world like a magnet, but none succeeded. It only saw its second ascent over a year later during the visit of the incredibly fit Australian 'boy wonder' Geoff Weigand, who finished it off on the second day! (Does this say something for having 'beta' information about the route?)

The third ascent was made when the visiting British climber, Andy Pollit, completed it after only three days of effort, in 1991. This is in contrast to his much commented on 30-day attempt on 'Punks in the Gym' on nearby Mt Arapiles just prior to his visit to Stapylton.

Subsequent ascents have led to a controversial regrading of the route as 29 in the latest route guide. However, much of the protection, including jammed wires and cams, is now in situ, and so the original grade is probably more accurate for the first ascent.

There is no disagreement, however, on the fact that this is still a bold and extreme undertaking up 'the hardest wall in Australia', and that it remained the hardest mixed-gear route in the country for a good few years.

The Indian Face – Mt Snowdon

A red rag to a sitting bull

NO BOOK THAT PURPORTS TO INCORPORATE rock climbing can exist without including Wales, 'where it all began' (*American Climbing Magazine*, May 1995). The tradition of hard, somewhat insane, natural-gear protection really did have its beginning here, and continues. Few climbers will not recognize the names of Geoffrey Winthrop-Young, Colin Kirkus, John Menlove-Edwards, George Mallory (of Everest fame), Chris Preston, Joe Brown, Don Whillans, Nat Allen, Jerry Moffat, Ron Fawcett, John Redhead and more recently, Johnny Dawes. All have had a tremendous influence on the rising standards of rock climbing, all have been bold, and all have left their mark on Welsh climbing.

Wales has a wonderful olde worlde charm. Perhaps it is due to the gently winding roads and meandering stone walls, the verdant, sheep-dotted hills, or the quaint slate-roofed cottages. One would feel quite unsurprised by a road sign proclaiming: 'Here be Goblins'.

Underneath the apparent gentleness of the Welsh, however, lies a hardiness born of the climate and the stone. For it is the stone that has shaped them – the quarries, the coal mines and the hills. Climbers do not stay long before the toughness seeps into them, and the routes in Wales reflect this. The traditions of hard, sparsely protected climbing live on in the creations of the contemporary rock artists.

Clogwyn Du'r Arddu, or 'Cloggy', represents the best of the Welsh (to be fair, UK) climbing. It is a large, lonely chunk of rock perched high on Mt Snowdon, the highest point in Wales (and England). The cliff towers up for 65m (215ft), split at two-thirds of its height, on the left, by a grassy ledge. It has been the scene of many outstanding climbs, but also controversy, particularly the Great Wall, or Eastern Buttress. Its history reads like a Who's Who of climbing. The route up the Eastern Buttress was put up by Alfred Piggot in 1927 – it is aptly known only as Piggot's Climb, and at VS (Very Severe) was quite a landmark at the time. The next epic feat is probably Joe Brown's unbelievably bold and futuristic Vember, an E1 put up in 1951 with Don Whillans. Pete Crew's Great Wall, established in 1962 at E4, was the next route of significance, being the first one to break out onto the huge, featureless central slab, now recognized as the area of Cloggy (Great Wall was fully free-climbed in 1975 by the 17-year-old John Allen, in keeping with the tradition of 'hardy youths'). In 1978 Pete Whillance and Armstrong led The Midsummer Night's Dream, a bold line that sweeps across the central slab, using a tiny bit of Great Wall to reach the stunning top pitch. Pat Littlejohn and Terry King cut into the top of the crag with The Axe in

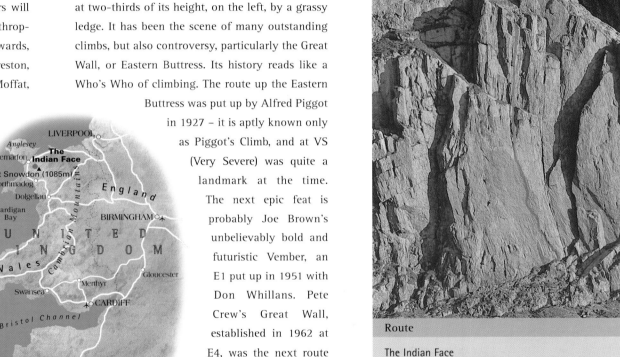

Opposite Johnny Dawes of the UK precariously placed in a highly charged position, way above his nearest marginal protection points. A fall from this point would certainly be disastrous.

Route	
The Indian Face	
Grade	
E9/6c	
Area	
The Great Wall, Clogwyn Du'r Arddu, Mt Snowdon, North Wales	
Length	
65m (215ft)	
Date of first ascent	
4 October 1986	
Climber	
Johnny Dawes (UK)	

1979, and in 1983 Jerry Moffat, the 'wonder boy' of British climbing, broke out onto the main slab with his somewhat arrogantly named Master's Wall, the first E7 in the world.

For those unfamiliar with UK (and to some extent, European continent) climbing, the plethora of routes on Cloggy is bewildering; what is a 'new route' in between all these lines and bits of line? In the UK in particular, there are thousands of keen climbers, and a very limited amount of rock. It is not surprising to find climbers squashed together, or sharing pieces of other climbs to reach virgin territory.

The climber

Briton Johnny Dawes started climbing as a 14-year-old, and soon was pushing hard routes on the Sheffield gritstones. In 1984, at 21 years old, still looking like a fresh-faced schoolboy, he established Braille Trail, an unbelievable E7/6c at Burbage, with Gaia at Black Rocks following two years later (both in the Sheffield area).

Nineteen eighty six was his 'highlight year' – during this, among many other routes, he put up an E8, End of the Affair at Curbar; Come to Mother, an E7 on the sea cliffs at Gogarth; The Quarryman, E8 on the Dinorwic slate quarries (unrepeated to date); and of course The Indian Face. The very range of these climbs shows his amazing versatility, ranging from hard, powerful boulder problems on gritstone to the flaky rock at Gogarth; the blank, featureless slippery slate at Dinorwic to the fingery, balancey, desperate climbs at Cloggy. Johnny regards The Quarryman as one of his best routes, despite it being a thrusting, grunting, strenuous climb up a blank open book in the depths of a man-made slate quarry. The top pitch is the supposed crux (7b) but the third pitch is the one that Johnny seems made for – a series of contortions and full-body moves that throw other climbers off like the proverbial water off a duck's back. Most climbers simply shudder when they look at Dawes's routes, knowing that to fail on most of them means serious injury or death.

The route

The very centre of the Great Slab lay untouched. Many climbers had abseiled down the area, and gone away shuddering at the lack of protection. One bolt would have solved the fear problem – but placing a bolt in this shrine of hard, traditional climbing would have been considered very unethical by the British climbing circuit.

The Indian Face really revolves around the Master's Wall route. This itself has a stormy history – the main protagonists being John Redhead and Jerry Moffat, two of the leading lights in the 1980s. John Redhead climbed The Master's Wall line, but placed a bolt (with the subsequent – expected – high controversy) about halfway, and retreated (in the words of Moffat,

'like a dog pissing to mark his territory'). Redhead called the short route The Tormented Ejaculation. Moffat abseiled down, chopped the bolt, and then proceeded to lead the 'necky' route all the way to the top, renaming it Master's Wall, doubtlessly irritating Redhead beyond belief. Moffat's lead was the first E7, and took Welsh (and some may say world) rock climbing to a new level of commitment and difficulty.

Indian Face starts off on the 'easy' E7 Master's Wall pitch, to a rock overlap where two small flakes allow a bridging rest, then onto a leftwards-leaning groove. The climb then deviates left onto the blank, overhanging section, the real 'meat' of Indian Face. This starts in two faint grooves, moves

past a small overhang onto a long line of tiny flakes, followed by the famous 'mantelshelf' and the blank slab that exits onto the Master's Wall finish. In its initial form, the only protection on this 20m (65ft) section was a tiny peg behind a loose flake, in reality no more than a psychological help. The route then takes to the Master's Wall, finishing up the E2 pitch of Jelly Roll.

The flake on Indian Face provided even more Redhead controversy – during an abseil down Master's Wall after the opening ascent of The Indian Face, Redhead supposedly pulled lightly on the peg, which 'just came out in my hand'. Discovering that the flake was 'dangerously loose', he (in the words of High, 1987) 'returned with Dave Towse and abseiling together, they removed the offending piece of rock, carefully carrying it to the bottom of the crag and all the way to Llanberis and bravely delivered the flake to Johnny Dawes, which was like waving the proverbial red rag to a sitting bull.' This led to Dawes's subsequent thumbing his nose at them via his May 1988 ascent done without the flake – a brave (and some may say foolhardy) gesture indeed, but one which proved without doubt that he was the best and the boldest climber in the country.

The climb

A superb tongue-in-cheek route description comes from *Welsh Rock*: 'The climbing is on holds unremittingly exiguous in nature – their paucity proving such a drain on mental facilities as to daunt the heart of a would-be leader, even though he may be the stoutest of fellows. Protection is at best illusory; the whole sweep of rock affords not so much as a single nubbin on which the thinnest line may be secured ... should the leader fail to negotiate the crux, or be seized by a palsy high on the pitch, disaster must be imminent.'

'I can do it, I can do it, I can do it on paper!' exclaimed Johnny Dawes, after retreating from an early attempt. 'It's no good doing it on paper, Johnny, you're going to have to do it on the rock', the late Paul Williams, who was watching, commented laconically.

The Indian Face did not go easily. Johnny Dawes inspected the route on abseil a number of times, including locating potential gear placements ('There were none!' said he). Eventually, on

Indian Face, Mt Snowdon, Wales

4 October 1986, he was ready. Conditions were right – dry, but cool, with no wind. Even a breath of air could have disturbed his balance, dislodged him from the tenuous grip he had on the face.

Johnny, a poetic and articulate soul, likened his climb to playing with high voltage equipment – a false move, and it would mean 'a jolt to the heart'. He said '…as you move higher, the voltage grows, and amongst the myriad connections there lie false trails that can kill'.

On this first ascent, Johnny entered the crux moves too hastily, and nearly tipped off the rounded boss after the key mantelshelf move. 'If I fell off, the gear would rip, as it was to the left and could only take downward-pulls.' He somehow managed to hold his balance, and to clip the tied-off RURP (Realized Ultimate Reality Piton – a minute few centimetres of thin metal). He 'rested' on the tiny ledge for a while, then went for the next crux, a move over a slippery, rounded bulge onto three tiny crystals for the right hand.

With only this tenuous grip, Johnny skipped his feet to effect foot-swaps a number of times to avoid leg cramps – a precarious move at the best of times, let alone high up on the most difficult climb in the world! One mistake, and the hands would not have held. 'There is no resting. I must climb and go for the top. I swarm up towards the sunlight, gasping for air. Fearful of a smear on nonsticky boots, I use an edge and move up, a fall now fatal.' (Johnny Dawes) Ignoring a 25m (80ft) fall that was threatening on a single tiny RP1 (a minute metal wedge), with a series of powerful side-clings, pulls and lunges Johnny moved up and onto the 'easy ground' of Master's Wall. The Indian Face, climbed in the Indian summer of 1986, E9/6b–c (USA 5.13a) had been completed – the first, and for a long time, only, E9 in the UK.

What makes a relatively short route like Indian Face so extreme? A mountain guide friend asked to define an extreme climb, said, 'Doctor Death has to be there looking over your shoulder – mess up, and you're his.' The Indian Face certainly fits the bill.

Left Johnny Dawes finds an almost impossible bridging rest before tackling the delicate crux moves.
Opposite Redhead's symbolic painting, which replaced the controversial 'kidnapped' flake.

Total Eclipse of the Sun – Wales

Pushing the edge of deep-water soloing

THE CARDIFF AREA OF SOUTH WALES IS certainly not the place one would choose for a warm summer sea-cliff climbing holiday. It is a windswept, rugged area, characterized by high cliffs and wild water. The Bristol Channel has water which is both cold and murky, the latter making it difficult to spot any rocks that might lurk below. The tidal range is fairly large (up to 9m/30ft at spring tide – or rather, at total eclipse time. . .), but the region below water is full of jagged rocks, which can lie within 1m (3ft) of the surface or less than that, even at full tide.

Ogmore is well-known and loved in climbing circles for its numerous spectacular routes of all grades that lead up its chunky limestone rock. There are some real test pieces through the Tiger Bay roofs. A good number of the climbs, both roped and solo, were pioneered by chalk-cliff guru, Pat Littlejohn (director of the International School of Mountaineering in Leysin, Switzerland) or by Martin Crocker, many in the early 1980s. Littlejohn's traverse Bigger Splash was the first major route in the Tiger Bay area.

Approaching the cliffs during normal tide, one passes over a multitude of broken outcrops of rock, with which the aspirant soloist would do well to get acquainted. These are the features that radically affect the 'landing zone', and on occasion 'pinpoint landings' based on a thorough study of these have been all that has prevented disaster. The Tiger Bay area is some 40m (130ft) in height, and is dominated by the large sea cave in its centre. Like all sea caves, when the tide is running, the water inside is choppy and extremely dangerous, with strong undertows pulling this way and that.

The climber

Martin Crocker has been a part of the British climbing scene for a long time. His playground has been the south of Wales, where he put up a good number of the routes at Ogmore and other sea cliff areas. Of those which were done by others, he invariably did the first repeat ascent. Martin frequently soloed routes which others had put up in conventional style, and his boldness in climbing high above the choppy waters has led to the nickname (little used in his presence – despite his mild manner, he is not a man to be trifled with!) of Crazy Crocker.

There is little doubt that no-one knows the position of the underwater dangers better than Martin, which doubtless is the reason for his survival remaining intact over the past 15 years of outstanding climbing and new-routing.

Route	
Total Eclipse of the Sun	
Grade	
E8 (crux F7b+)	
Area	
Ogmore, South Wales	
Length	
200m (660ft) traverse	
Date of first ascent	
August 1999	
Climber	
Martin Crocker (UK) – free solo	

Opposite Briton Martin Crocker nearing the end of the first long crux above the initial overhang. Here the water under him is only a few feet deep with jutting rocks perilously close to the surface. This is the extreme edge of deep-water soloing.

Right A pensive Martin Crocker just after completing Total Eclipse of the Sun – possibly wondering how he had done it!

The route

After a successful few days of soloing a number of extremely testing routes, such as Mantra (E5/6a), Sorcery (E6/6b), and putting up Buzzarena (E6/6c or F7b+), Martin felt ready to prepare for his project – a full traverse of the Tiger Bay zawn (cave) and cliff. This was set to coincide with the freak tides expected with the total eclipse. During the day of the eclipse he abseiled down to place some water on the tiny perch of a route called Warlock just before it enters the zawn, which would allow him a much-needed break on the traverse. As the tide started to reach its zenith, and the sun began to sink

rapidly towards the horizon, he started his evening of tension. The traverse starts at the left-hand edge of the cliff (viewed from the sea) by down-climbing the Siren chimney to a point some 12m (40ft) up the huge cliff. The intimidating traverse starts at 6a, then rapidly jumps to intricate F7b+ traversing on the lip of the large roof – 8m (25ft) above the sea, which is only a few metres deep at that point. After this comes a rising traverse to the left-hand corner of the zawn, which is totally undercut, at F7b+ once again. A sideways pull-up move onto the minute Warlock stance led to a much-needed water break with the preplaced bottle. Now into the dark depths

of the cave – not perhaps as technically exacting as the previous cruxes, but mentally more mind-blowing. 'Below lie monsters' – in this case, not the sharks and sea-beasts of our imagination, but the rocks and swirling undertows of the zawn. Slowly the route moves right onto blanker, still undercut ground, then a slippery move onto a set of jugs 12m (40ft) above the (all-too-shallow) sea. Thereafter, it is 'simply' a case of climbing the trade route Fire for the 30m (100ft) to the top.

The climb was largely on-sight, the only pre-inspection being the second crux, which was inspected on abseil from 'way out in space in front of the cave'. Although Martin had climbed many of the routes touched by the traverse, no-one had ever entered much of the territory he covered.

Martin took 35 minutes to complete the solo. The photographer, Carl Ryan, described it as the most 'nail-biting first ascent' he had ever seen. This was not 35 minutes of combined effort, then rest, then effort – it was 35 minutes of pure hard climbing, with only one very brief water break. Without doubt it ranks as one of the great adventure achievements of the 1990s. One wonders whether anyone will have the patience to wait for the next total eclipse (in 2090?) to do a repeat ascent...

Opposite Martin Crocker committed to the down-climbing section which leads to the rest point on the extreme right, before the climb traverses into the gloomy depths of the zawn. At this point, although the moves are individually easier, the traverse is largely overhanging and the rock is greasy with sea-spray.

Above Crocker heading into the cave – the ominous roar and hiss of the surging current below serve as constant distraction to the rapidly tiring climber, making absolute concentration essential.

Right High above the sea on the overhanging moves out of the cave traverse, which lead onto the final 'easier' vertical exit section of the marathon route.

Ice & Mixed Climbing

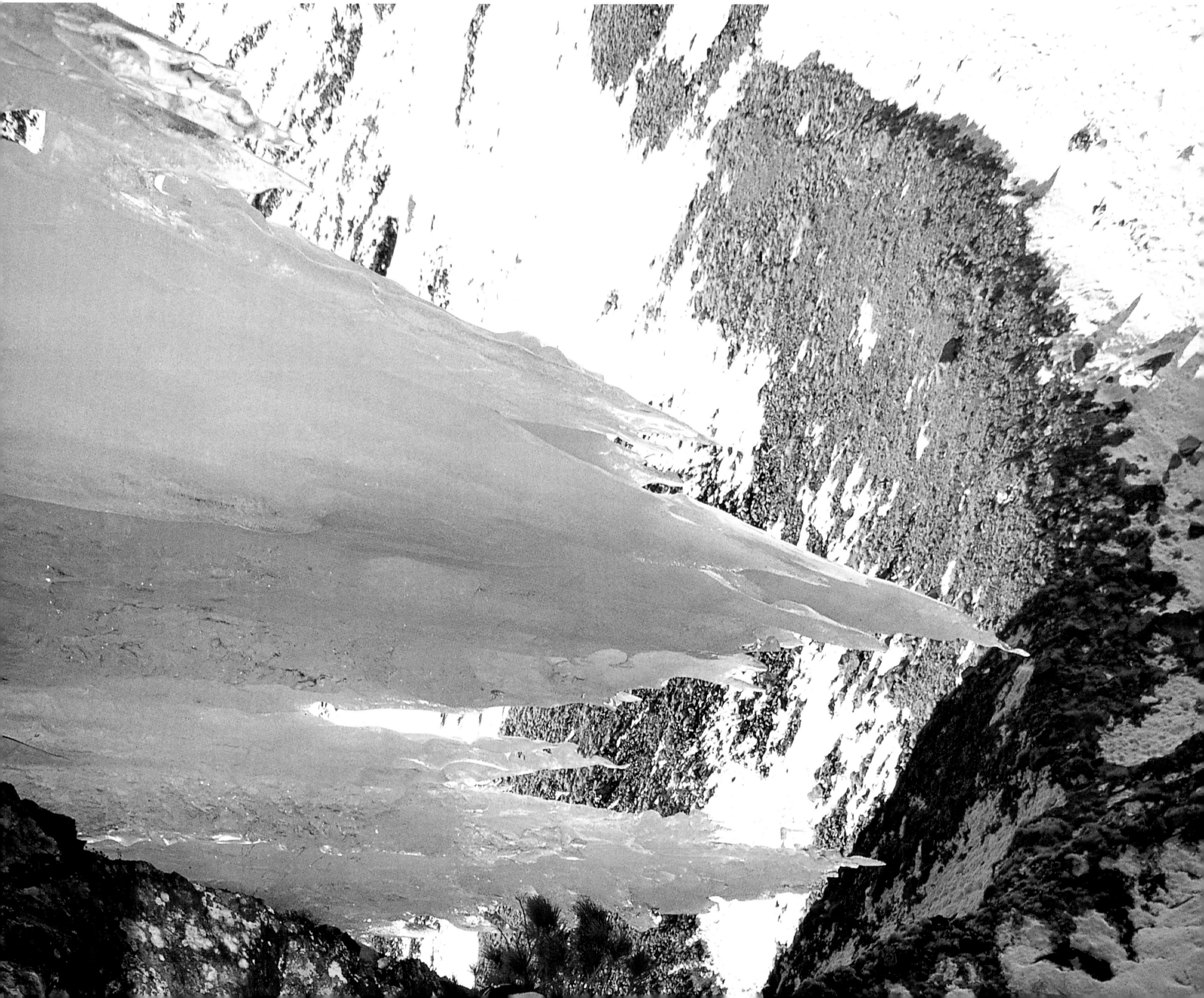

Ice & Mixed Climbs

The Great White Fright. X-Files & The Empire Strikes Back. Metanoia. Sea of Vapours.

CLIMBING STEEP OR VERTICAL ICE CAN be exhilarating, and many ice waterfall climbs are aesthetic in the extreme. They also tend to be rather terrifying, as it takes a while to get used to the idea that fragile-seeming ice can stay attached to the rock face even when it overhangs, and that 25mm (1in) of ice plastered to a sub-surface can hold one's weight. The grading of ice routes can be rather arbitrary, since ice re-forms at least once a year. Some of the more well-known routes are pleasantly consistent, and vary little from season to season; others can be totally different.

Ice climbing is done with the aid of crampons which attach to rigid boots, usually made of leather or special plastic. The front points of the crampons do most of the work on steep ice, although very new designs with single front teeth or 'banana-shaped' crampons with lateral teeth for hooking on steep icicles have made it possible to climb features that only recently were unclimbable.

The other important tool is the ice axe, used in pairs. The angle of the toothed pick on the axe is crucial, with different angles being suited to different tasks. The weight and balance of these short axes can be critical, and newer designs have taken current technology to the limits. On pure ice, the climber protects himself by placing ice screws – externally threaded metal tubes which get screwed into the ice and into which the climber clips the rope by means of a carabiner. Occasionally nuts, camming devices or preplaced bolts are placed in adjacent rock, adding protection. Other protection involves wrapping slings around 'icicles', drilling two holes in the ice which meet up under the surface to take a 'thread', or placing precarious metal-toothed hooks known as 'bull-dogs' (the latter often as psychological protection).

Pure ice climbing is rare in extreme climbing. Most modern extreme ice routes involve climbing on ice that is thinly plastered over rock, or lies in a crack in the rock face, and sections where there is unformed or no ice are tackled as rock pitches – an interesting experience, as this is usually done in crampons. Known as mixed climbing, it has its origins in Scotland – where much of the techniques and equipment were developed – and in the European Alps. This genre gained hugely in international popularity after the ascent (and associated publicity) of Mixed Master in the Canadian Rockies by Troy Kirwan and Joe Buszowski in 1991.

In 1975 the Burgess twins and Bugs McKeith had approached the adjacent Polar Circus – which had a hanging ice pencil on the upper reaches – from the side and climbed it, a feat far ahead of its time. This pencil touched the base mushroom in 1991, leading to numerous bottom-to-top ascents. These climbs caused climbers to stop focusing only on completely formed ice pillars and sheets, and to tackle 'futuristic' routes which consisted of drips or smears of ice, and hanging ice pillars. This is the type of 'thin' route described in Sea of Vapours.

A second trend has been long, serious routes, such as Metanoia, which is a true 'mixed' route in that the stretches of ice are separated by equally long stretches of almost pure rock climbing, including some of the most serious aid climbing ever done. It is included here as it was a winter route, and the rock was invariably plastered with ice.

Previous pages Stevie Haston, from the UK, dry-tooling his way towards the icicle on the M11 second pitch of The Empire Strikes Back, Val Valeile in Italy, currently considered one of the hardest mixed routes in the world.
Opposite, left to right First ascent of the X-Files; Haston on The Empire Strikes Back; despite the climber's equipment and the appearance of the picture, this is not ice but the top pitch of the chalk horror Great White Fright, Dover, UK.
Right The late Alex Lowe (UK), highly revered for his mixed ice climbing, on Les Misérables, Alberta, Canada.

The Great White Fright – Dover

The domain of the lunatic fringe

CROSSING THE CHANNEL FROM EUROPE TO England for arrival at Dover, one cannot fail to be impressed by the band of gleaming white that hoves into view as the ferry nears the port, and to be stirred by the stark, unique beauty of the cliffs. As the ferry draws closer, these vertical cliffs tower high above it on both sides of the harbour, with a steep road winding down in the one area where they do not abut directly on the water. They are the famous white cliffs of Dover, immortalized in song, for aeons a landmark for sea-farers. The conglomeration of the skeletons of millions of diatoms that make up the cliffs stretches for over 36km (22 miles), offering plenty of challenge for those climbers bold enough to attempt to breach their ramparts. The cliffs are chalk – an unconsolid-ated form of limestone, and, as such, a friable and to many unappealing medium on which to climb. During World War II, the warden of the watch for Dover is reputed to have said, 'What – put troops on top of them cliffs? They must be crazy! Only a lunatic would try to get up that way'.

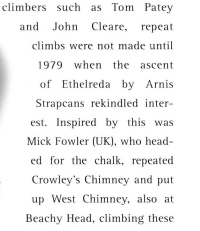

The cliffs

Most climbers would maintain that chalk cliff climbing *is* the domain of the lunatic fringe, bear-ing out the warden's argument. Perhaps it is fitting that one of the early adherents was the notorious and highly controversial Aleister Crowley, who called himself 'The Great Beast, 666'. Crowley was an eccentric of the first order, but was also an exceptional climber. As early as 1883, he put up a new route on the legendary Napes Needle in the Lake District in northern England and, between his devil worshipping, managed to co-lead the K2 expedition in 1902, which reached 6584m (21,602ft) – not exceeded until 1938. On the chalk cliffs of Beachy Head in 1894, Crowley put up Devil's Climb, Crowley's Chimney and Ethelreda's Pinnacle. Despite attempts by climbers such as Tom Patey and John Cleare, repeat climbs were not made until 1979 when the ascent of Ethelreda by Arnis Strapcans rekindled inter-est. Inspired by this was Mick Fowler (UK), who head-ed for the chalk, repeated Crowley's Chimney and put up West Chimney, also at Beachy Head, climbing these in traditional rock climbing style. A comment after the ascent was, 'It's really quite simple – you've just got to climb it faster than it crumbles.'

Fowler's next move totally altered the face of chalk climbing. Along with Chris Watts and Andy Meyers he climbed Dry Ice, at Dover, using crampons and ice axes. An incident occurred when the coast guard and police responded to hysterical calls about 'people in trouble on the cliffs' and repeatedly tried to force an at first bemused, then irate, pair of climbers to be rescued.

Phil Thornhill now joined in on the chalk activ-ity, and between him and Mick Fowler (with odd incursions by the likes of Pat Littlejohn and Andy

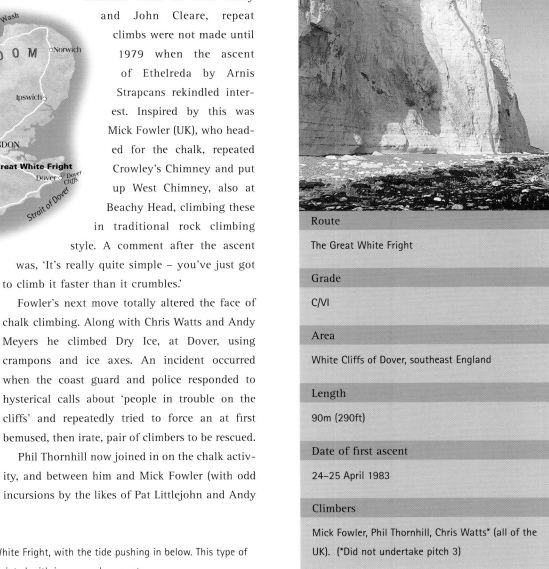

Opposite Phil Thornhill of the UK on the first pitch of The Great White Fright, with the tide pushing in below. This type of climbing draws very few adherents, largely due to the danger associated with insecure placements.

Route	
The Great White Fright	
Grade	
C/VI	
Area	
White Cliffs of Dover, southeast England	
Length	
90m (290ft)	
Date of first ascent	
24–25 April 1983	
Climbers	
Mick Fowler, Phil Thornhill, Chris Watts* (all of the UK). (*Did not undertake pitch 3)	

Meyer) opened a host of new lines using the 'Dover mixed technique', which consisted of dry-tooling with axes up the crumbling chalk, mostly in crampons. Protection was via 'warthogs', a form of lightly serrated solid ice spike. In 1984 Phil Thornhill, climbing with an equally nervous Victor Saunders, put up the incredible girdle traverse, Reason to be Fearful – 1260m (4150ft) of sideways climbing near Hastings, which was completed in six visits over three months.

In 1989, Mick Fowler, with Steve Sustad, put up 'The silliest route on the silliest cliff ever climbed...', a 145m (475ft) rock climbing traverse with one pitch at Grade 6a (the rest of the grades being 'ungradable' mixed chalk-rock pitches).

Dave Pegler, of the UK, describes the chalk cliffs as being '... like no other rock. It requires great coolness, good ice technique, a wacky sense of humour, a willingness to break the rules and an adventurous disposition'. Small wonder that there are so few chalk aficionados!

Since the early 1990s, a good number of routes in a variety of grades have been climbed in a wide range of styles, from good old-fashioned 'traditional' rock climbing on standard protection (requiring a very long neck!) to the more modern 'chalk sport climbs'.

It is this last form of climbing on chalk that has produced a great deal of controversy – Dave Pegler, climbing the 1992 traditional route Exlax (a name that reflects the feelings of many chalk climbers) in the Pleasuredome, decided to leave the warthogs used for protection in situ. Each time one is removed from the blocky, broken chalk, large chunks break off, altering the nature of the route and making it more difficult for subsequent ascensionists to place gear. 'Why not leave it in place?' he asked.

Added to this were the problems climbers were having obtaining placements at the often heavily weathered and rotten limestone at the top of the cliffs, and the odd skirmish with the authorities patrolling the clifftop paths (climbing is not actually illegal on the chalk, but officials often do not appreciate this). The result has been a series of new routes which are almost 'sport' routes in that they have preplaced gear (nowadays even placed on abseil), many 'top out' on warthog anchors far below the actual clifftop, and the routes are redpointed, that is, practised until the climber can

eventually complete the moves in one continuous go. Activists such as Dave Pegler, Neil Gresham, Tim Emmett and Leo Houlding (see p97) are pushing the limits with climbs such as Gresham's Massive Attack (C7), Emmett's Mr Plastic Man (C8), Pegler's Transvision Ramp (C6–7) and Houlding's as-yet unnamed and uncompleted roof problem (C9?). Most of this activity is concentrated in The Pleasuredome, a hugely overhanging sea-cave 'like half of St Paul's Cathedral dome', some 36km (22 miles) from Dover. This cave overhangs 15m (50ft) in 45m (150ft) of height.

Unfortunately routes on chalk can't be guaranteed – like ice routes, they change rapidly, and routes such as the famed Orgasmatron (C8) by Pegler and Gresham no longer exist, having fallen down!

The climbers

To describe Mick Fowler as a 'prolific' climber is to understate his achievements. His pedigree is given in more detail on p136 (Spantik). His role in the chalk-climbing scene has been both embryonic and developmental – after three decades of climbing, he is still there, pushing the limits.

Phil Thornhill put his considerable climbing talents, and extremely bold disposition, to work on the chalk after his ascent of The Birds with Andy Meyers in 1981. He followed this with a solo ascent of the frighteningly loose Escape Hatch at Dover – the only way to escape a rapidly incoming tide! Thornhill put up 20 hair-raising routes in 1982–83, many with Fowler, some solo, and self-belaying when his second refused to follow him! His magnum opus was of course the traverse at Hastings mentioned above, after which he 'retired' to complete his PhD – although he has returned and remains an active new-router.

Chris Watts left the sport of motorbike racing to take up climbing, with his first incursions being in the company of Mick Fowler and Andy Meyers. He proved to be a talented and versatile climber who frequently left the security of London to head for the wild hills of England and Scotland.

The climb

Literally a stone's throw from Dover harbour lie the steep, high cliffs of St Margaret's Bay. Some 2km (1.5 miles) eastwards, a notable prow sticks out, a bulging arête with an overhanging top section. This is the steepest chalk band in the immediate Dover area, and was the obvious challenge to Fowler and crew. The climb was done in '1980s new fashion' – ice axes and crampons, with warthogs for protection.

It is quite an experience climbing the chalk in this way – the cliff faces the sun, and climbing can be done in T-shirts or even shirtless, while wearing gloves, normal to prevent the hands being bashed on ice, is not the best idea in the heat. April was warm enough to force the team to adopt a different method – they taped up the axe leashes with thin foam to prevent them cutting into their wrists. Climbing in jeans and heavy boots complete with crampons provided quite a spectacle.

The trio started up just left of the arête, and moved directly up for 5m (15ft) to a ledge, when they were forced to cross the arête onto the right where a shallow groove gave a modicum of protection. After this, the route moves onto the gently overhanging arête to a good belay stance 30m (100ft) above the sea – plenty of space between the feet!

The second pitch trends leftward, following the sinuous arête, which turns into a precarious overhanging ramp, necessitating some delicate climbing, protected by warthogs, bulldogs and skyhooks. This finishes off on a superb-looking stance, a huge pillar – which unfortunately tends to move slightly underfoot. Although this is the shortest pitch (22m; 70ft) it took a few hours to sort out the intricacies of the route.

The final and longest (40m; 130ft) pitch proved to be the hardest. Chris Watts took one look at the loose, blocky, overhanging beast, and decided to ˙.. head for home while I can still get there. . ˙ The team abseiled off, and Mick and Phil returned the next day to complete the climb.

This was Mick's lead, and it turned out to be ˙..one of the best pitches anywhere..˙ (Dave Pegler). The pitch is totally unrelenting – it starts off with strenuous moves up the overhanging wall above the stance, then moves rightwards to below some wild overhangs. Using torqued axes in a thin crack, Mick moved onto a grey section of chalk, which brought him up via a less steep but still overhanging shield of rock on the right of the main overhang, onto the final headwall.

What makes this route, and this form of climbing so special, was the way in which it was done. There was no pre-inspection, the climbers moved onto totally new territory where there was strong possibility that they might not find solid enough anchor points for an abseil if the route proved impossible and they had to retreat. All protection was placed on lead, often while the leader was dangling precariously on overhanging ground from a single shallowly embedded ice-axe tip, crampons scratching away at the friable chalk. Large blocks kept dislodging, making the belayer thankful for the overhanging nature of the climb, but adding to the tension for the leader. Despite all this, the climb was done in fine fashion – no resting on aid, no hang dogging, no pulling on gear, with long and dangerous lead-outs being preferred to resorting to aid.

In the final analysis, what is chalk-cliff climbing? Is it merely rock climbing with ice tools? Is it a form of mixed climbing, such as the Scottish winter routes? Or is it just another strange form of insanity, best left to the modern Aleister Crowleys? It is certainly an ephemeral form of climbing since the routes change year by year as pieces fall off, weathered by wind, sun and wave. The Great White Fright was a landmark route in terms of difficulty and style of ascent; no two ascents will ever be the same.

The Empire Strikes Back & X-Files – Val Valeile

'An unearthly creation that scares people'

VAL VALEILE AND VAL DI COGNE LIE NEAR THE town of Lillaz in Italy. Val Valeile joins Val di Cogne, a long, winding and beautiful valley with steep river-cut sides. In winter, the countless small waterfalls from the surrounding mountains freeze into a spectacular and appealing set of long icefalls in the valleys. The area has become popular with European and overseas climbers in the past few years, and a recent icefest held there has further increased its fame.

The climber

Stevie Haston is a British climber who has spent the past few years based in Chamonix, France, where he can pursue his three loves: alpinism, snowboarding and his wife Laurence Gouault-Haston – photographer, fellow-climber, belayer and confidant.

Stevie is an amazing all-rounder, with a number of incredible achievements to his credit in fields as diverse as sport climbing to big walls and big mountains. These include sport routes up to 8a (Pourquoi Pas in Buoux and Hegel in Volx); Sans Liberté, at 8b+ the hardest rock route in Chamonix; 60-odd solos in the Alps including the Frendo Spur at the tender age of 16, the Super Couloir on Mont Blanc in two and a half hours, the Bonatti Route on the Dru, and the first winter solo of the Walker Spur.

He ascended Shivling in 1990, and again by a new route, the West Ridge, in 1995. In ice and mixed climbing, Haston also has a formidable list of achievements, from countless repeats to first ascents such as The Terminator (the first Grade 7 ice route done in Wales), as well as Fatman and Robin (M8+) in Vail, Colorado, and Welcome to the Machine, first Grade 9 in Italy. When it comes to total, breakneck, lunatic commitment, tempered by experience and professionalism, he has no equal, be it on rock or ice.

The routes

Choosing to combine the two routes here may seem a little odd. It is not that either is not worth a section on its own, but rather that the two, having been done in the same valley, by the same climber – one in the old millennium, one begun in the old and completed in the new – makes a compelling pairing.

In January 1998, Haston saw an ice cascade that made him gasp – 'The route is a dream or a nightmare . . . your heart and your soul are drawn to it, it hangs in space like something from another world.' This 100m (330ft) of ice broken by short sections of rock was X-Files, named after the television series because 'it was an unearthly creation that scares people, like the show'.

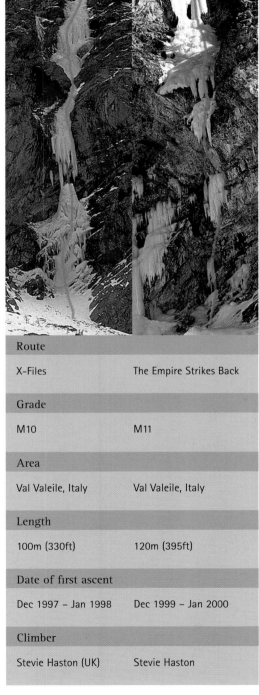

Route		
	X-Files	The Empire Strikes Back
Grade		
	M10	M11
Area		
	Val Valeile, Italy	Val Valeile, Italy
Length		
	100m (330ft)	120m (395ft)
Date of first ascent		
	Dec 1997 – Jan 1998	Dec 1999 – Jan 2000
Climber		
	Stevie Haston (UK)	Stevie Haston

Opposite Stevie Haston coming up to the Ice Curtain. The extremely overhanging nature of the climb is evident in the angle of the ropes as well as the climber's body. 'Torqueing' the axes into cracks is the best way to get any purchase.

The climb was eventually graded M10 (mixed ice, Grade 10, making for a numerical pun in the ranking); it was at first a contentious grading in a sphere of climbing where most ice climbers had not even touched a Grade 9 – but one that was borne out by subsequent ascents.

Just less than two years later, the valley ice-falls were once again in fine form, and Haston spied a new and equally impossible-looking line within sight of X-Files. This line, longer, steeper and more fragile than X-Files, was inspected and partially equipped from adjacent routes as December 1999 drew to a close. The first pitch was done in the old millennium, but the rest only completed in January 2000, to open another science-fiction-named climb, The Empire Strikes Back – recognized as the first M10 in the world. Italian Maura 'Buba' Bole, who did the second ascent, is convinced that it rates M11; he called it 'suicidal', quite an acclamation from one who has opened numerous M8 and M9 climbs, and re-peated most of the major mixed test-pieces in the world. His ascent was unfortunately incomplete, as the third pitch had already fallen down.

X-Files

Stevie Haston had been eyeing the line of X-Files for a few years. It was only in 1998, after his sea-son in Vail, Colorado, where amongst other wild routes he completed Amphibian (9a+) in a day, that he felt ready to tackle the fragile, overhang-ing and dangerous-looking set of ice fins, pillars and icicles that make up the climb. There would be little or no room for error on a route such as this, with no possibility of retreat short of a suicidal jump from the overhanging ice sections.

The first pitch went fairly easily to someone of Steve's calibre – 50m (165ft) of good, cauliflower

ice, which led to another 50m overhanging pitch. This was the crux pitch, and took three days to equip, including a number of serious leader falls while he was moving up it. The first 25m (80ft) mixed section was climbed on a combination of rock and tiny fragile icicles, with a modicum of protection possible on the rock behind – five shallow pegs and five hand-placed bolts.

The second half, a huge icicle hanging out in space, was climbed totally without protection, as Haston felt that any rope drag caused by the protection during a fall would result in his ropes being cut by the sharp fins and tubes. On the photo shoot, Haston took a huge fall, during which a large fin of ice did slice through one of his ropes, proving his point. The ice sections were climbed without practice or close pre-inspection, to maintain the committing nature of the climb.

The climb was repeated by American Will Gadd, who confirmed that it was harder than the then world test piece, Amphibian. The route was also repeated by Buba Bole, who took a long fall while dry-tooling (pulling on ice axes lodged in rock cracks) on the second pitch. He claimed it to be an almost unjustifiably risky climb.

The first female ascent was made by Canadian climber Kim Csizmazia in 1999. She is the first woman to climb Grade M10, placing her way ahead of her nearest female rivals, and a long way in front of most ice-climbing men.

Perhaps the most poignant thing about ice routes is their ephemeral nature – the plastic medium of ice flows differently from year to year, ascents made in one season can differ totally from the next. It is this that excites the creative ice enthusiast. He knows that no two performances will ever be the same; each dance will be unique, every repeat a new challenge.

Opposite left An absurdly fragile set of icicles plasters the rock in this, the most insane form of mixed climbing, on the crux pitch of X-Files.
Opposite right Briton Stevie Haston – one of the boldest and most innovative of modern climbers.
Right Haston smacks an ice tool in and pulls around the lip, his belayer visible far below. Despite the cold, Stevie prefers climbing 'bloody and bare-handed' to enable him to 'fiddle in the protection' more easily.

The Empire Strikes Back

In December 1999, the Val Valeile drew Stevie Haston back like a magnet, to examine a line that everyone had declared 'impossible' or 'outrageous'. A relatively easy climb just adjacent to his proposed route gave him a chance to examine it at close quarters, and he decided that it would possibly go, but only with some preplaced gear at key points on the first two pitches.

It took a few days to equip these from the adjacent route – two bolts on pitch one, a two-bolt belay, and five bolts and a peg on the second pitch. Watery ice, falling rock and ice, and some

Above Like the proverbial Sword of Damocles, fragile shards of ice guard The Empire. Moving from the illusionary security of rock onto the fickle ice is the most trying part of this sort of climbing.
Opposite Onto the second pitch (M11): less ice, more overhang, sparser protection (is this rock climbing, or ice?). Tremendous forearm strength is needed here.

leader falls all added to the delay and the difficulties of pre-equipping the climb.

Haston was scared that the fragile-looking third pitch wouldn't last long, so decided to climb it first, before returning to Chamonix for 'New Year, a rest and training'. He moved onto it from the adjacent route and climbed it in a matter of a few hours, claiming it to be 'only Grade WI7, but X for fragility, death totally certain if it detaches, like some weird tribal initiation rite'. There was no protection from the second belay point to the third belay, 20m (65ft) above. To bear out his fears, the entire huge stalactite did detach, but fortunately only when he was taking his break in Chamonix.

On returning, he tackled the first pitch, a superb but scary Grade M8+/9. The first belay point was a dangerous one, with loose ice and rock frequently tumbling down onto it. The second pitch was the real test – a series of thin ice scoops, flakes and overhanging icicles precariously and randomly attached to the rock. There was no real continuous ice on this extremely difficult mixed-

ground section, which had to be climbed with axes switching from 'hooking' on tiny rock projections to delicate, tip-only placements in thin ice. Crampon points had to be placed precisely on these tiny edges, or carefully chipped in to the ice smears. Sometimes Haston had to lovingly wrap his legs around a fragile column of ice, or handjam between ice and rock. In many cases, way above any solid protection, a fall was unthinkable, the consequences too harsh, and only Haston's iron control kept him going. The section eventually succumbed to repeated nerve-wracking attempts, allowing him to redpoint it at Grade M10+. The two top pitches were pleasant grades WI4 and WI5, the 'finale' being up a magnificent, solid, semi-detached ice pillar – a grand way to finish a momentous climb.

The route was repeated (without pitch 3) by Buba Bole in February 2000, confirming the grade of pitch 2 as M10+, possibly M11. Will Gadd was quick to get in the third ascent, also grading it M11, and claiming that it was 'the hardest and most dangerous climb I have ever done'.

Metanoia – Eiger

Mixed paranoia from the Master of Ice

THE BERNESE OBERLAND, THE AREA OF HIGH mountains in Switzerland falling in the Bernese Alps, is dominated by the Jungfrau-Mönch-Eiger trilogy. The longest glacier in the Alps, the Aletsch, drains these peaks. The chocolate-box Swiss valleys lie below, rich in green meadows, tinkling cowbells and glorious scenery. It is a beautiful and consequently highly commercialized area, with cable cars feeding skiers and hikers high into the hills.

The Eiger Railway which ploughs straight through solid rock for many kilometres to the Jungfraujoch is a well-known tourist attraction, and cuts out the long slogs that were the lot of early climbers in the area. The rock is largely limestone, with a fair sprinkling of gneiss. This combination tends to make the rock passages on climbs friable, often with loose chunks. The area is popular with climbers of all standards, the ultimate prize still being seen as the somewhat notorious North Face of the Eiger.

The peak

The Eiger is probably the most widely known of all Alpine peaks, partly because of its somewhat macabre history of death and drama, largely because of exposure in a number of books and films, one of the more recent being the dramatic thriller, *The Eiger Sanction*. The peak has three major aspects: the southwest flank, the northeast face, and the northwest (or North Face, as it is known). The latter is referred to as the Eigerwand (or often as the Nordwand – or Mordwand, death face). The North Face is composed of broken dolomite for the lower two-thirds, capped by a layered, black, crumbly and slatey gneiss above. It is a huge cliff by any standards, with its 1800m (5900ft) face of near vertical rock, ice and snow.

The Nordwand of the Eiger seems to breed its own weather – this face lies on the fringes of the Bernese Alps, and catches the brunt of incoming storms and disturbances. In addition to major fronts, the abrupt, vertical nature of the cliff and the bowl-shape of the face also create microcosmic weather patterns which can, and do, catch many climbers unprepared. The face is split midway by large icefields, with very steep rock characterizing the two flanks and the top.

The history of the North Face is well-known to most climbers. Several of the leading lights of the 1930s had died while trying to break the back of the looming Nordwand, largely because nationalism and the threat of war was putting pressure on climbers to solve the problem. In 1935 Max Sedlmayer and Karl Mehringer made the first serious attempt, and were watched with interest via telescope from the hotels in the valley below. The watchers were disappointed as bad weather closed in, and when it cleared some days later, the pair was nowhere to be seen. Their bodies were later seen from the air, and the Death Bivouac high on the face was named. One year later,

Route	
Metanoia	
Grade	
5.10/A5/M6	
Area	
North Face, Eiger, Switzerland; 3970m (13,026ft)	
Length	
1800m (5900ft)	
Date of first ascent	
March 1991	
Climber	
Jeff Lowe (USA) – solo	

Opposite Well-equipped American Jeff Lowe, still fairly low down on Metanoia, recovering from the rigours of the pitch he has just completed. At this stage he is gathering strength and getting organized to haul the heavy kitbag up to his stance.

Toni Kurz set out with Anderl Hinterstoisser, Edi Rainer and Willi Angerer. They crossed the now-famous Hinterstoisser traverse, a long, difficult, smooth section of rock, then pulled their rope – a fatal mistake, as it made retreat across this section nigh impossible. Angerer was struck by a stone close to the Death Bivouac, and they were forced to retreat. Weather closed in, and the Hinterstoisser traverse proved impossible to cross in reverse. In abseiling down, Anderl came off, and pulled the rest of the party from their precarious stances. The rope broke, plunging all but Kurz to immediate death. He hung suspended, injured, cold and desperate, a few metres above the rock window which opened into the Eiger Railway tunnel. In full view of the watchers in the hotels below, desperate rescue attempts were made, but failed in the face of high winds, difficult ice and sleet. Kurz died of exposure a scant few feet from warmth and safety.

In 1937, six unsuccessful attempts were made, and yet another climber died. Two teams were rescued, although there was much official and even more media-generated hype about dangers to the rescuers. In June 1938, two Italians, Bartalo Sandri and Mario Menti died just above the Difficult Crack, still low down. The other hopeful contenders in the valley below were shattered, and a few teams left the scene.

In mid-July two groups started virtually simultaneously – Austrians Fritz Kasparek and Heinrich Harrer, and Germans Anderl Heckmair and Ludwig Vörg. Eventually, despite much drama and near-death accidents, the foursome, now climbing together, made the summit on 24 July 1938. The victory was somewhat overshadowed by political furore when the German pair was honoured by Adolf Hitler – only weeks away from the start of World War II.

The North Face lay in peace while the world lay in chaos. After the war, the route was unrepeated until 1947, when Lionel Terray and Louis Lachenal made it through the face of an awesome lightning storm. There were a number of repeats before the 13th party died in 1953. Climbing stopped on the Nordwand until the controversial rescue of Claudio Corti and Stefano Longhi, and the mysterious disappearance and deaths of Günther Nordrift and Franz Mayer. The face was quiet again until the 1960s, when a number of tragedies and a few successful repeats reaffirmed its difficult nature. The first three solo attempts all led to deaths, and the great Italian, Walter Bonatti, had the good sense to retreat from his attempt ('No Mountain is worth as much as one's life'). It was finally soloed by Swiss guide Michel Darbellay in 1963. Ascents by Gaston Rebuffet, Don Whillans and Chris Bonington (they halted halfway to rescue a fellow climber, McNally) once again brought the face into the public eye, renewing interest in the Nordwand.

In 1966, the so-called 'last great problem of the Alps', a direct line up the vast North Face, was attained by an unusual combination of climbers, and under tragic circumstances.

Much like the first ascent, two groups of climbers arrived at the same time, with the same object. An American-British party, with Dougal Haston, Don Whillans and Chris Bonington (all of the UK) led by the then-director of the International School of Mountaineering in Leysin, John Harlin, with fellow American, Leyton Kor; and a German team of Günther Strobel, Roland Votteler and Siegfried Hupfauer, led by Jorg Lehne. Both groups had chosen to climb in winter, to reduce the dangers of stonefall and avalanche, but each had a different approach. The Germans were going to siege the face in almost Himalayan fashion – fixed ropes, digging snow caves, and with many carries of equipment up and down. The others were set on a fast, Alpine-style ascent, with a minimum of gear and as few fixed ropes as possible. This was not to be – bad weather sent them jumaring up and abseiling down the ropes to the warmth and comforts below a few times. It was during one of these jumaring sessions that a fixed rope gave way just below the infamous 'Spider' icefield, and John Harlin was killed. The two groups combined to finish the climb, and named it the Harlin Route in John's honour. At ED3–4, the route is extreme.

In 1969 a most controversial route was sieged by a six-person Japanese party, consisting of Michiko Imai, Takio Koto, Yasuo Kato, Susumu Kubo, Hirofumi Amaneo and Satoru Negishi. The climb took one month, and hundreds of bolts were placed. In 1970, Hans Berger and Hans Müller climbed the route Alpine-style, without using the bolts.

The first female solo ascent of the North Wall, by more or less the original route, was made by Catherine Destivelle of France (see also p76) in 1992. In the interim, American Jeff Lowe had established his mega-route, Metanoia.

The route

The Harlin Route takes a gradual swing from the left of centre of the North Face across to the centre at the level of the second icefield. From there it meanders a little, but not excessively. Jeff Lowe was determined to straighten the line, and strove for the true *diretissima*, the Cassin definition of 'the path a drop of water would take from the summit to the base'. This is in fact what Metanoia does – from slightly right of the summit, the route plunges straight down to the second icefield, moves slightly left, then drops in a straight line to the base, with a tiny deviation at the top of the Shattered Pillar. In the upwards direction as opposed to the description of the drop, the route shares a common start with the original (Heckmair) Route and the Japanese Route up to the top of the easy climbing on the

Shattered Pillar, from where it angles leftwards, thus moving in below the Hinterstoisser Traverse, which it joins on the left (completion) of the traverse. Common ground is then shared up the Ice Hose for a short section, after which the route crosses the second icefield and takes a completely independent line up the steep slabs of the top half of the North Face.

The climber

Jeff Lowe has been variously described as the Guru and the High Priest of ice and mixed climbing. He possibly might disagree with the mystical connotations, being of a largely practical nature, but few would disagree that he is the Master of the Art. Jeff is one of the originators of many of the techniques and tools (such as Hummingbird tools and Snarg ice pitons) that are the stock in trade of the extreme ice climber. He admits to starting climbing at age seven with his father, on no less an ascent than the Grand Teton in Wyoming! At 15, ice climbing started seriously, and the ascent of the Harlin Direct in 1966 was one of his major inspirations. His list of significant ascents is so huge as to stagger one. To mention but a few: the first solo ascent of Bridal Veil Falls in 1970, the 1500m (5000ft) ice climb on the North Face of Kwangde in 1982 with David Brashears, the northwest face of Kantega in 1986, the north ridge of Latok in 1978, and the Yugoslav route free on Trango with Catherine Destivelle in 1990. He did the first M8 and M9 routes in the world.

In addition he has been one of the main movers behind sport-climbing competitions in the USA, including the well-known Snowbird Lodge, and is of course a prolific climber on rock and ice.

The climb

In March 1991, Jeff arrived in the Lauterbrunnen Valley somewhat ill at ease with himself as a result of the failure of his business and his marriage, but determined to fulfil a long-standing dream, a new route on the Eiger. Perhaps he felt that a statement of some sort was needed, and doubtless memories of the great Bonatti solo attempt on the Dru after he returned, frustrated, from his K2 experience inspired Jeff to go for the largest, most feared face in the Alps. 'I thought that doing the Eiger alone in winter by a new route, the hardest yet, would be as close as I could get to the level of commitment of the original pioneers.' (Jeff Lowe, as reported in *Conversations with Climbers*, by Nicholas O'Connell)

Lowe was determined to do the route in style – and to him, this meant predominantly no bolts.

Opposite The 'Master of Ice' attacking an ice pillar – unphased by the long lead-outs on precarious placements.

Above The awesome sweep of the icy North Face, with the Mittelegi Ridge visible on the left of the photograph.

Deciding that to establish a new line on the crumbly, easy rock on the lower sections would be almost an insult, he started off on the 1938 line, climbing this as far as the top of the Shattered Pillar in a few hours. A few moderate pitches followed, bringing him to the steep, overhanging section leading up to the termination of the Hinterstoisser Traverse, some 200m (650ft) higher. This section of rock was ice glazed, and devoid of easily climbable features. There were a number of tenuous cracks, and the 'mixed master' tackled these head on.

The crux pitch proved to be one which demanded more than 30 continuous metres (100ft) of A5 aid – standing and relying on 'hooking', that is, using tiny metal hooks that merely rest on a projection or in a pocket in the rock as the sole means to move. The grade of A5 is only given when there is no chance of survival after a fall – in other words, a death fall would result from any mistake, and ropes would be of no use as the protection was absent or inadequate to hold a falling climber. In solo climbing, this is made even more difficult as there is no partner to carefully pay out slack – the leader has to drag the rope through the auto-belay system himself. There is also no comforting word of encouragement, no 'Go for it, mate!' There is only the howling of the wind, the panting of one's own breath, the pounding of the heart.

The best part of two days went by, with seven hours spent on the crux pitch alone. A thankful Jeff ended up on a bivouac ledge on the smallish icefield adjacent to the Hinterstoisser, but at this point he was forced to descend, having experienced constant problems with his ice tools.

After sorting this out, he reascended, lugging his 30kg (66 lb) haul sack with him. After the first rock band, he decided it was much easier to carry 20kg (44 lb) on his back, the rest dangling from his harness between his feet. This lasted as far as

Left In this section the rock is so steep that the snow does not adhere to it. Sections like this forced Jeff to resort to aid climbing at difficulties of up to Grade 5.
Opposite Perched like a human fly on the final ice gulleys which lead to the summit ridge, Lowe almost disappears in the immensity of the frozen landscape.

the end of the second icefield, after which he resorted to standard techniques – climb the pitch, abseil down, fetch pack, re-climb or jumar.

The next section gave some excellent mixed climbing, which Jeff graded as M6 – about as difficult as one can get! This consisted of partly consolidated ice on friable rock, with the occasional good ice-filled crack which allowed him to 'torque' his axes in. Difficult choices constantly had to be made: to wear crampons and reduce efficiency on the rock or to risk slipping on the ice underfoot on the ice sections. Whatever he did, it seemed always to be the wrong choice. There were huge sections which consisted only of delicate face climbing on limestone. 'I had to use eight anchors on tiny little things, all equalized, to set up one belay. From there I looked up and went, 'Where do I go from here?' So I just started wandering up these little limestone edges, mixed free and aid, doing whatever I could to get up.'

Bivouacs were mostly in his tiny bat tent, but Lowe describes trying to sleep in this 'like trying to sleep in a cement mixer' – referring to the numerous spindrift avalanches that kept on descending on him.

The final section allowed for far more free climbing, with superb pitches succumbing to standard climbing techniques, but at the grade of a staggering 5.10 – a level of difficulty seldom reached in the Alps, and incredibly impressive at this altitude under winter conditions. The ever-present cold can sap the energy of the climber, and the constant up-and-down and pack-hauling necessitated by solo climbing can drain the will. 'I was climbing about as hard as I could climb. I took three falls on the climb . . . because I was climbing at my limits and popped. I've never done that in the mountains before.'

The ascent took a total of nine days – the two days before the first descent, and seven subsequent to resuming his high point.

Metanoia ranks as one of the hardest, most extreme routes ever done in the Alps. It is the only Grade A5 in Europe, to which is added 5.10 free rock climbing, and M6 climbing – and all of this done solo by Jeff Lowe, and in winter! A truly bold and audacious attempt, which can certainly be equated to the exploits of great Italian Alpinist, Walter Bonatti, and all of the original pioneers.

Sea of Vapours – Rockies

Climbing frozen mist in an alien landscape

THE CANADIAN ROCKIES COVER A HUGE expanse, and include some of the finest ice and mixed climbs in the world. The endless sea of peaks can be almost depressing. Where to begin? Where to end? How to find the routes?

The key areas for ice climbing are to be found in and around two major national parks – Banff and Jasper. These are close to the 'Rodeo Town' of Calgary, and are well-served by roads and even highways. There are literally thousands of documented routes in the area. Despite the apparent accessibility, the Rockies are still very much wilderness. Avalanches are the single biggest danger, and take a good number of lives each year. Temperature variations can also be hazardous – Arctic fronts which move in at great speed can cause temperatures to plunge from a pleasant 1° to -30°C (34 to -22°F) in a few hours. Most climbs are from one to five hours' walk from the nearest access road, and the days are short in winter. Rescue is difficult to arrange in bad weather, thus any accident can become life threatening.

Mt Rundle is the dominant feature of the Banff National Park area, clearly visible from the Trans-Canada highway. No section of the mountain is more avidly watched by the ice-climbing fraternity than the section of the brooding north-east face, now called the Trophy Wall, which includes one of the finest concentrations of challenging ice routes in the world. The mountain is split at about one-third of its height by a huge rock band, topped by broken snow slopes. Right of the middle of this band is the Trophy Amphitheatre, which holds legendary names such as Replicant (145m/475ft; V/WI6+) – done by Keith Haberl, Joe Josephson and Tim Pochay in 1994; The Terminator (150m/500ft; V/WI6+) – opened by Craig Reason and Jay Smith in 1995; and Sea of Vapours (165m/540ft; V/WI7+) in 1993.

Worth a mention is Troubled Dreams (WI6+/M8) – the variant by the original Replicant crew, freed by the legendary Alex Lowe of the USA in March 1996 (he later died in an avalanche on Shishapangma). The rapid progress of modern ice climbing can in some ways be seen in this area. Sea of Vapours was way ahead of its time, and is still considered to be a full-on 'modern' route. Replicant followed in 1994. It is named after the clones in the film *Bladerunner*, which lived their lives so intensely that they were burned out after a short time. The first pitch is the crux, with a wildly overhanging finish on thin ice and having little by way of protection. 'Falling off is not an option,' according to Canadian Joe Josephson. Replicant set the standards for climbing fragile, partly formed ice pillars and ice smears which are only occasionally connected to the rock.

The Terminator has only properly formed twice: 1995 and 1997. The first ascent took two days, and was given a controversial Grade 7 (it was soon

Route	
Sea of Vapours	
Grade	
V/7+/R	
Area	
Mt Rundle, the Rockies, Banff National Park, Canada	
Length	
165m (540ft)	
Date of first ascent	
February 1993	
Climbers	
Bruce Hendricks, Joe Josephson (both of Canada)	

Opposite A pair of Spanish climbers nears the top of Sea of Vapours, which was in prime condition in 1997. The ice in the foreground is the top of Terminator, another great route in the Trophy Wall area of Mt Rundle, Canada.

downgraded to 6+). On this route, the first 30m (98ft) is climbed on a free-hanging 'giant icicle', approached by getting the axe tips to lodge on the very bottom of the pillar, then swinging one's feet onto it from the rock on the left side.

A later party came in from rock behind the ice flute, starting at the frightening grade combination of A2/WI7/X. The second pitch climbs a

Lacelle stunned the climbing world by free soloing the entire set of climbs – a landmark event in ice-climbing history.

The climbers

Joe (Jo-Jo) Josephson is a Calgary resident, but not a rodeo rider – he is a technician, who spends every free minute in the mountains, preferably on ice. Best

Bruce Hendricks, a lecturer at Calgary University, is perhaps not as well known as Joe, but is nonetheless a bold and ardent ice climber. Some might say that anyone who climbs with Joe has to be both of these. Joe, on the other hand, claims that Bruce taught him the art of this madness. Hendricks, too, has a number of excellent first ascents to his credit, including his first solo ascent of Blessed Rage (200m/650ft of Grade V/5.7/WI6) in 1992. Sea of Vapours in his opinion still stands out as the finest of his routes.

The route

When one reads about the ice climbing described above, it might leave one cold for entirely the wrong reasons. After all, the routes are only some 160m (520ft) high, and surely it is just a case of whacking the axes in, standing on the crampons, and plugging on up the route? What's the problem?

Sea of Vapours (the name comes from a landmark on the moon – it was 'like climbing frozen mist in an alien landscape') was perhaps the first truly 'modern' ice route that made use of tenuous, fragile, disconnected sheets of thin ice. Climbers had previously stuck (no pun intended) to the solid sheets, runnels or pillars of ice which were firmly attached to the rock, until the boldness of Josephson and his compatriots took hold.

In rather unusual conditions in February 1993 a frightening but compelling line of ice appeared in the Trophy Wall area, joining onto a short climb called Postscriptum. Barry Blanchard, James Blench and Bruce Hendricks attempted the line, but were repulsed on the second pitch. A few days later, Bruce returned with an enthusiastic but somewhat nervous Joe Josephson. The 45m (150ft) of Postscriptum is used as the first pitch of Sea of Vapours, up to a hanging belay. This pitch fell to Joe, who warmed up slowly in the early morning on this 'known ground'. The second pitch at Grade 7+ moves off rightwards on extremely thin, technical smears of ice which hardly seem to be adhering to the underlying rock. This was the real crux pitch, which Bruce had led on the first, aborted, attempt. The brittle ice shattered into tiny fragments on each placement of the axes, and it seemed inevitable that the thin, fragile ice would peel off the rock. 'After hours on the pitch, I was drained emotionally, to the point of exhaustion'. (Hendricks)

fragile, free-hanging ice curtain, then the climb eases off a touch to the top, although it remains vertical to mildly overhanging.

The logical extension to this extreme ice-climbing circus was a linkage (enchaînement) of the whole triplet of routes, which was first done in February in the exceptionally fine early 1997 season by Keith Haberl and Ken Whylie, with François Damilano and Guy Lacelle repeating this feat a few weeks later. On 18 March 1997 Guy

known as the author of the guidebook Waterfall Ice – Climbs in the Canadian Rockies (those who know him wonder how he found time to write this. . .), he is a consummate climber, and as bold as they come. Many have been known to refer to this boldness as 'craziness'. An impressive number of hard first ascents bear witness to his creativity and fearlessness, and he has climbed with all of the other 'big names' in ice climbing. He is regarded as the 'guru' of Canadian Ice, and not without reason.

Gradually Bruce's confidence returned, and he moved up to find a fairly good belay point, a single number 4 stopper, 40m (130ft) above his anxious belayer.

The second time around, Joe Josephson was persuaded to lead this, with the advantage of a few more ice screws that Bruce had taken along. This time Bruce jumared up the pitch, to save time.

The third pitch was slightly more solid, although this is all relative! It finished up with a hanging belay on a number of solid placements – security for the climbing pair at last! The final pitch was once again given a 7+, leading off over a fragile mushroom-like overhang onto smooth vertical ice to the top. Just before this, Bruce dropped one of his axes, and (somewhat embarrassed) had to borrow Joe's to lead the pitch.

All of the belays are hanging belays, mostly on friends and nuts. This, the lack of protection on the long and serious pitches, and the technical, 'thin' nature of the ice is what made the Sea of Vapours an instant sensation. It pushed the limits of the possible, and was given a grade of 7+, the first of this calibre grade in the world. (Grades of 7+ were officially awarded to other routes only as late as 1999, giving some idea of how far ahead of its time this 1993 route really was.)

The designation 'R' in the grade description stands for 'Run-out' or 'Risky' – the inference is that there is little by way of protection, and any error would be more than serious. The climb is both physically and emotionally draining, and no-one would argue that Sea of Vapours is a route to be respected.

The bold efforts of Joe Josephson and Bruce Hendricks redefined the meaning of 'difficult' in ice climbing terms, and forced other climbers to push their own limits further than they had dreamed possible. By their example of boldness and commitment, Joe and Bruce brought about a host of new and difficult climbs.

Opposite left Hazardous smears of ice on Sea of Vapours.
Opposite right Joe Josephson on the crux, pitch two.
Right Josephson on the second pitch of Replicant (145m/475ft; Grade 5). Sea of Vapours branches off lower down, and takes the thin ice smears and pillars on the right-hand side. ,

Alpine-scale Climbs

Weg Durch den Fisch. Destivelle Route. Divine Providence. The Gift.

'I live life passionately; there is great pleasure in this and that takes care of everything'

Catherine Destivelle after her solo ascent of the Petit Dru

THIS STYLE OF CLIMBING HAD ITS ORIGINS IN the European Alps, but has spread to the most remote regions of the world. The concept differs from its closest relatives, rock (and ice) climbing and expedition (and big-wall) climbing, in a number of ways. The first and most important is that the climber carries with him or her all the equipment necessary to complete a climb which stretches, or potentially could stretch, over a number of days.

In normal rock and ice climbing, the climber does not expect to be out for more than a day, thus if any bivouac gear is carried, it is for pure emergency and in consequence is very sparse. In big-wall or expeditionary climbing, loads are ferried up and down the mountain or wall, the climbing party does not carry all the gear needed for the whole climb. The alpinist by contrast has to be totally self-sufficient on a route that may, by accident or design, stretch over more than a day. The other difference is that alpinism usually involves at least an approach over snow and ice, even though much of the climbing is usually done on rock.

Within the realm of modern alpinism are major variations on the above. Many alpine routes can be and are finished in a day, particularly with cable-cars, ski approaches and descents, and improved equipment. At the other end of the scale, alpine-style climbing is now being applied to the Himalayan and other 'giants', where it is becoming accepted that moving capsule-style, carrying minimal bivouac equipment with no sub-camps or porters, is a commendable way to tackle even very hard routes at altitude.

Alpine-style ascents require a high degree of competence in the climbers. Not only do they have to cope with objective hazards (crevasses, séracs, snow, weather and rockfall) but speed is often of the essence for completion of the route, or for survival. A variety of skills are needed, including rock climbing, snow and ice climbing, and bivouac skills.

The routes given here as Alpine-scale offer a good overview of the variety to be encountered. Divine Providence is perhaps the most classical case of such an ascent, done in excellent style.

The Fish (Weg Durch den Fisch) is a route in the Italian Marmolada, not really considered to be the true Alps. It was done in traditional alpine style, that is, self-suffcent movement over a number of days, and has a snow and ice descent, although the approach lacked this element.

Frenchwoman Catherine Destivelle's route on the Dru is a true Alpine experience, though it was in many ways also a big-wall climb, and in this case, done solo, with an unusual form of descent!

Unlike the other three, which are located in the European Alps, The Gift That Keeps on Giving is an Alaskan climb. It totally fulfils the requirements for an extreme alpine climb, showing the way in which contemporary hard climbing is done. Elsewhere in this book, there are cross-over routes, such as Ship of Fools, which is classed as a big-wall route although it was in essence a prolonged alpine-style ascent. Similarly climbs in the Big Mountain section could be classed as alpine style as none used porters on the actual route, although high subcamps were used in a few. The best description for these would, however, be capsule-style climbs.

Previous pages American Steve House on pitch 4 of The Gift That Keeps on Giving, Mt Bradley, Alaska.

Opposite, left to right A climber carefully making his way across the Great Roof on Divine Providence; Catherine Destivelle, from France, perches high above the ground like a frozen fly on her epic solo of Petit Dru, Mont Blanc; absolute concentration is required on this ultimate route in the Italian Dolomites, The Fish.

Right A long lead-out without protection is par for the course on the treacherously smooth rock of The Fish.

Weg durch den Fisch – Italy

Scaling the heights in great style

THE DOLOMITES IS THE NAME GIVEN TO THE set of towers and spires composed of the many-featured sedimentary rock, dolomite (magnesium-based limestone); they lie largely in northern Italy (an area variously called the southern Tyrol, Südtirol or Alto Adige). They have played a key role in the development of climbing and climbing techniques in Europe and indeed the world.

The faces are large, alpine in scale, but often without the normal alpine glacier and snow and ice approaches in summer (winter climbing in the Dolomites is, however, truly an alpine experience). Their central position in Europe has made them a playground for many climbers, including the great names in climbing.

The Marmolada is often referred to as the jewel of the Dolomites. Perhaps it should be called the Crown – seen from a distance the mountain (in fact, more of a range) looks like a circular crown, with its 3km-long (2-mile) backwards-curving South Face. The Marmolada is probably the most stupendous of the dolomite walls. The grey and gold rock, 860m (2800ft) high, soars skywards in a series of awe-inspiring faces and towers, from just off-vertical to overhanging. The section below the Ombretta (3529m; 10,578ft) is the highest.

The nature of dolomite climbing is extremely varied, ranging from easily protectable cracks and chimneys to virtually unprotectable faces and slabs. The fairly soft (and in many cases friable) rock does not always lend itself to safe traditional protection with nuts, camming devices and pegs. This has led to the temptation to drill or glue in 'solid' metal bolts, particularly in the last few decades. Many climbing activists feel that bolts diminish the value of the experience by reducing the risk factor to negligible. The South Face of the Marmolada is one of the regions where climbers are actively fighting against the excessive use of bolts, in order to retain the bold, committing nature of the free climbing.

The South Face

The South Face was a much sought-after prize, and it is significant that the first route established on the face proper was by a party led by a British woman, Beatrice Tomasson, with her guides M Bettega and B Zagonel. They climbed the original route at the dawn of the new century, in 1901. The 650m (2100ft) route was a landmark achievement – it was the hardest route (IV+) to be climbed in Europe at that stage, and a profound statement in favour of female climbers. It was done by a little-sung woman, who climbed a staggering array of bold routes without seeking glory or even recognition. For Beatrice, climbing was done for its own sake, and that was enough.

The winding and twisty earlier routes gradually made way for the more direct lines, such as the Südtiroler Weg (VI/A0/A1) of Reinhold Messner

Route	
Weg durch den Fisch (The Fish)	
Grade	
VII+/A4; free at IX-	
Peak/Height	
Marmolada, 3342m (10,965ft)	
Area	
Marmolada Ombretta, Italian Dolomites	
Length	
850m (2780ft)	
Date of first ascent	
August 1981	
Climbers	
Igor Koller, Jindrich Sustr (both of the Czech Republic)	

Map labels: Switzerland, Bolzano, **Weg durch den Fisch**, Mt Marmolada (3342m), Matterhorn (4478m), Slovenia, France, Turin, MILAN, Verona, Venice, Croatia, Po River, Genoa, Bologna, Bosnia Herzegovina, Gulf of Genoa, Apennine Mountains, Ligurian Sea, Pisa, Adriatic Sea, Corsica (France), I T A L Y, ROME, NAPOLI, Sardinia (Italy), Tyrrhenian Sea, Palermo, Sicily (Italy)

and Kurt Renzler, done in 1969. Messner, along with Enzo Cozzolino and Manolo (Maurizio Zanolla), was outspoken against the 'frivolous use of bolts, which eliminated the word impossible from a climber's vocabulary.' They preferred to climb without them where they could. Many climbers, however, still resorted to aid in order to bypass difficult sections and save time. This included the use of pegs and hand-drilled bolts, sometimes to an extreme degree, creating virtual bolt ladders that were condemned by the local climbers.

In 1981 two Czech climbers, Jindrich Sustr and Igor Koller, grabbed the bull by the horns – or rather, the fish by the tail – and took the most coveted line, up the huge 860m (2800ft) slab that dominates the centre of the South Face to give Weg durch den Fisch (The Way Through the Fish, but known simply as The Fish).

The next climb of significance was that of Heinz Mariacher and L Iovane, aptly called Modern Times. The 800m (2600ft) climb was done in 1982 in impeccable style, pure free climbing up to Grade VII+ on very sparse gear and virtually no bolts.

This is now proving to be the way to go in the Dolomites – free, pure ascents of older aid routes, offering the modern climber a worthy challenge in the face of ever-shrinking virgin rock on which to establish new routes of significance.

The ultimate goal is perhaps still that of a clean, free, natural protection, on-sight ascent of a route. For many of the hard routes on the South Face of the Marmolada, that is the challenge awaiting future generations of climbers.

The route

The Fish takes an impressively direct line up to the cave called the Eye of the Fish, in the middle of the otherwise featureless slab that dominates the highest part of the South Face of the Marmolada, exiting near the Ombretta cable station. It is a route of unrepentant boldness, which could easily have been tamed by a profligate use of drilled-in bolts. Fortunately for climbing, the first ascensionists were aware of the almost sacred nature of the piece of rock, and were determined to ascend it without defiling it with fixed protection.

The climbers

After many years of cutting his teeth on climbs in the High Tatra in what was then Czechoslovakia, Igor Koller made his way west to the Dolomites. There he found a rock different to the granites he was accustomed to, but much to his liking.

The entire nature of Czech climbing was one of boldness – there simply were neither the funds nor the variety of protection equipment available, so a 'hard man' approach was essential. This transferred easily to the friable dolomite rock, which needed climbers with the ability to stand the pressure of long run-outs on very little gear.

The Fish was only one of many superb routes to Igor Koller's credit. The most recent of note were Viva Gorby (Grade VIII), put up on the Marmolada di Penia in 1991, and Rain From a Clear Heaven (VIII) on the Ombretta.

The pedigree of Jindrich Sustr reads much the same as that of his compatriot. When opportunity allowed, he frequented the Alps and the Dolomites. The Fish represents the high point of his career in alpine-scale climbing.

resorted to aiding on pegs or skyhooks. On some occasions, small holes were slightly modified to hold the skyhooks, allowing a series of delicate moves to be made on these.

As they moved higher up the face, a strange combination of tiredness and increasing confidence led to longer and longer, and bolder and bolder pitches. As mentioned earlier, the dolomite rock is very difficult to protect, unless one has a substantial crack system, or uses bolts. The climbing thinned out, and the pair had neither good cracks nor bolts to drill. They were following tricky sections, with small flakes and curving cracks breaking the tiny, finger-sized sculpted holes and pockets that characterize the open faces in the Dolomites.

This kind of climbing requires a cool head, and total commitment, with long lead-outs above scant protection making the consequences of a fall extremely serious. Blind-ending cracks had to be carefully and nerve-wrackingly down-climbed, and other options had to constantly be explored in order to make progress.

Some of the pitches were modestly graded by them as VII, though subsequent ascensionists gave the grade more as VII+ (the highest grade at that time). Similarly, the skyhooking aid pitches which they graded as A1 were regraded by later climbers as Grade 3 or 4. Possibly neither of them fully realized the extreme nature of what they were doing, nor (thankfully) were they concerned about the potentially fatal results of a long fall onto marginal gear placements. Suffice to say that later groups were in a cold sweat moving over the long 'hooking' aid sections which linked the lower two-thirds to the upper third of the route.

The weather held off, fortunately, as the pair were ill-prepared for extended bivouacs. In an effort to travel light, only the barest essentials were taken. Hanging bivouacs in slings were par for the course, and minimal food.

The third day saw a dehydrated and hungry but triumphant pair finally breast the summit ramparts, and abseil off.

The climb

Sustr and Koller, who had been doing routes in the Dolomites for a few seasons, had eyed the line of The Fish on a number of occasions.

The pair made their way to the base of the route, and overnighted right up against the rock face. Dawn saw them moving alpine-style, that is, fully laden with the minimum of gear needed if one expects to spend a few nights on an exposed rock face. The intention was to free-climb the route on nuts and natural gear, but as a backup they had taken a number of pegs.

From the start, the climbing proved far more difficult and dangerous than they had imagined, and they decided to use in-situ bolts from previous attempts and from incomplete or crossing routes to aid past some of the totally desperate sections. It is worth remembering that free-climbing was still a new art in the Dolomites, and aiding (even if only A0 – simply pulling on gear or standing on bolts) was regarded as normal. Wherever it looked possible to free-climb, they did, protecting as best they could; where not, they

Austrian Heinz Mariacher admits to being disappointed about this route being 'stolen' from him, under his nose so to speak, and was at first annoyed at the fact that the Czechs had 'abused' his route by using pegs, 15 bolts and skyhooks for aid. However, three years later, when he and Manolo finally repeated the route, he found himself both amazed and impressed. He was responsible for upgrading it to VII+/A4, and was outspoken in his praise for the young Czechs who had so unobtrusively stolen a march on many of the more well-known dolomite experts.

In 1987, Mariacher and Bruno Pederiva succeeded in redpointing the climb over two days. The route was graded IX-, making it the hardest climb in the Dolomites. Very few climbs exceed this grade even today, and even fewer of those are not fully bolted.

Opposite A long way down to the ground – Igor Pap jumaring up the 17th pitch to save time, in the summer of 1988.
Above left Igor Koller enjoying a strenuous section on pitch 5, during a repeat visit in 1991.
Above right Igor Pap and Rudolf Tefelner in the welcome Fish Cave bivouac; Monte Civetta looms in the background.

Destivelle Route – Petit Dru

Homage to Walter Bonatti

THE CHAMONIX VALLEY IN SOUTHEAST France, at the foot of Mont Blanc, is a climber's paradise. On both sides of the valley are countless large and small rock spires and faces, ranging from roadside crags for a quick after-work climb to high Alpine faces of many days' duration. Access is easy, via road, rail or *téléférique*, and the area is dotted with huts varying from tiny uncomfortable metal shelters to huge hotel-standard refuges. It is the playground of the wealthy who genuinely enjoy the mountains, and also the domain of the serious alpinist and climber. Many of the most noteworthy mountaineering feats have taken place in the few square kilometres that surround Mont Blanc, the highest point in Europe.

South of the valley, situated high above the little town of Montenvers, is the Petit Dru, a huge 1000m (3280ft) obelisk of tusk-shaped granite, its base at around 2730m (8960ft) above sea level. It slightly hides and overshadows its higher and larger brother, the Grand Dru, as the two project from the ridge leading up to the higher and equally difficult, but far less impressive, Aiguille Verte.

The peak

The Drus are highly visible from the valley below, and have tempted climbers for generations. The Grand Dru was first summitted by Britons Clinton Dent, Horace Walker and John Maund with the Swiss guide Alex Burgener in 1878; this was Dent's 19th attempt on the peak. Dent was in later life president of the prestigious Alpine Club.

The Petit Dru fell to three famous French guides, Jean Charlot-Stratton, P Payot and F Folliguet, a year later. But the sheer and difficult north and west faces of the Petit Dru were the real challenge, and they repelled all attempts until Pierre Allain and R Leininger climbed the North Face in 1935 at Grade VI/A2. In 1952 the next breakthrough was Guido Magnone's bold ascent of the West Face in the company of Laine, Dagory and Berardini. Then in 1955, Walter Bonatti stunned the climbing world with his six-day solo of the frighteningly steep southwest pillar, leading the way in individual commitment to major hard alpine routes. In 1962, Royal Robbins with Gary Hemmings opened the first 'American Direct' with a new direct approach to the Magnone Route. And in 1965 Robbins returned with John Harlin to open today's American Direct, a completely new and extremely difficult climb (now regarded as one of the best routes in the Alps). They showed the way in applying Yosemite aiding techniques to Alpine faces.

The last route considered to be of real significance before Catherine Destivelle's attempt was made by the Swiss-Czech Tomas Gross in 1975, when he soloed a line between the Bonatti Pillar and the American Direct in a three-week epic.

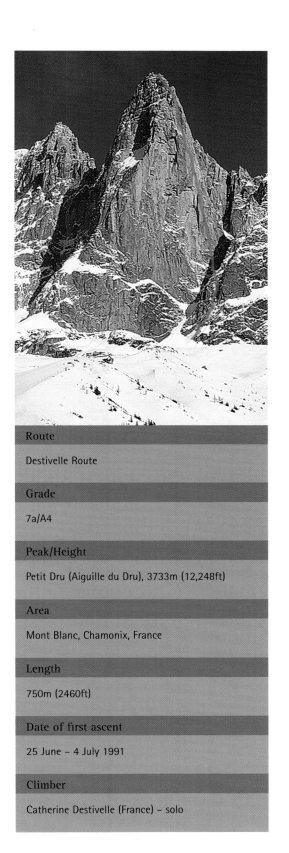

Route	
Destivelle Route	
Grade	
7a/A4	
Peak/Height	
Petit Dru (Aiguille du Dru), 3733m (12,248ft)	
Area	
Mont Blanc, Chamonix, France	
Length	
750m (2460ft)	
Date of first ascent	
25 June – 4 July 1991	
Climber	
Catherine Destivelle (France) – solo	

Opposite Is French climber Catherine Destivelle, seen here next to her portaledge bivouac, gesturing the helicopter away, or waving at the occupants? Her bold solo attempt generated a great deal of media interest, not all of it welcomed by her.

Alpine-scale Climbs

The climber

Catherine Destivelle of France is without doubt one of the most talented climbers to emerge in the last few decades. Without wishing to be at all derogatory about women in climbing, one of the leading editors of climbing magazines said, 'Even if she were a man, she would still be brilliant!' Catherine took no offence at this, admitting that men and women have different body and hormonal structures. However, she also made the point that female climbers are lighter and more flexible than their male counterparts – something which she has proven works to her advantage.

She started off bouldering in Fontainebleau at a young age, stunning the older male climbers with her prowess. Offers to climb came fast and furious, and she was soon in the French Alps, attempting major routes. By the age of 17, she had ascended the American Direct on the Dru in less than seven hours.

She then started a career in physiotherapy, and left climbing until in 1985 she was offered a star role in a film by Robert Nicod, which called for her to climb Pinchinibule in Verdon, France. At 7b+ (5.12c) this was the hardest route ever to be climbed by a woman, and after only six weeks of intensive training, Catherine was up to the task. Soon she was back in the thick of climbing, with competitions starting to dominate. She stayed in competition climbing, right at the top of the field, until this game began to frustrate her. She then joined Jeff Lowe (see p59) on a trip to the Nameless Tower in Pakistan, where they claimed the second free ascent of the Yugoslav route. This fired her enthusiasm for 'real' climbing once again, and she headed for the Bonatti Pillar on the Petit Dru as her first solo adventure.

Catherine had always admired – in fact, revered – Walter Bonatti, and admits that he was her role model in her early years. What started off as homage to her hero turned out a fiasco – she free-soloed the climb in just four hours, and the media had a field day. They made comparisons between her four-hour stint and Bonatti's six-day effort, denigrating the man she so admired.

Destivelle there and then decided to put up a new route on the Petit Dru, in order to experience first-hand the dangers and difficulties Bonatti had overcome. After her success on this, she went on to

Above Catherine Destiville hard at work amidst a jumble of ropes and haul bags. The weight of her sacks exceeded that of herself, and she described lifting them as a 'living nightmare'.

Opposite The rigours of the climb can be seen on Destivelle's face as she prepares herself for yet another difficult pitch on the superbly beautiful but unrelentingly steep granite face of the Petit Dru, Mont Blanc, France.

solo the Eiger and the Matterhorn north faces. To 'even the odds' brought about by equipment advances, she decided to attempt them in winter.

With her skills ranging across the board from competition climbing via sport climbing and alpinism to big walls, Catherine Destivelle has proven to the world that she is the finest all-round woman climber in history.

The route

Before heading onto the Destivelle Route, it is necessary to look at the route that inspired her effort. The Bonatti Pillar is still regarded by most as the key feature on the face of the Petit Dru. It is an obvious and elegant feature, which was just asking to be climbed when the young 24-year-old Walter Bonatti headed for it in August 1955. Bonatti felt he had something to prove to himself. He had just returned from the Italian K2 expedition, where he had played a vital but unrecognized role, and sacrificed his own chance of making the summit by taking supplies up to Lacedelli and Compagnoni. His role in this had been unjustly criticized, and Bonatti was feeling hurt and frustrated. The Dru provided him with the ultimate challenge. His climb was recognized as being a landmark in alpine climbing, and the young Destivelle read about and admired this feat in particular.

Destivelle sought out new ground as close to her hero's route as possible – not an easy task, as the Petit Dru had to a large extent been 'climbed out'. She realized that any new route in this area would need a good deal of aid, so she spent eight weeks in Yosemite with her friend and mentor, Jeff Lowe, mastering the complex advanced aid-climbing techniques. The climb in consequence takes what is not really a natural line up a series of cracks, expanding flakes, faces and chimneys between the Bonatti and Gross-Grenier routes, leading up over the smooth central slabs to the overhanging rock steps of the upper quartz band.

The climb

On 24 June 1991, with the help of some friends, Catherine moved her 65kg (140 lb) of gear into a bivouac site at the base of the great pillar. At 04:00 on the 25th she set off up the initial slabs, which went fairly fast, but soon gave way to pitches which could only be conquered on aid.

Pack-hauling proved to be her 'living nightmare' – she expected to spend six to eight days maximum on the route, and had taken food and water for this length of time. Along with the bivouac gear (which included a stretcher-like platform called a portaledge) and extensive protection, it amounted to a haul sack that was heavier than the climber!

From the second day, Catherine was plagued by snowfall. At first this was light, and no more than a nuisance, but the falls gradually became heavier and heavier, leading to extensive spindrift avalanches that soon had her cold and wet. There was very little free-climbing possible under these conditions, so she resorted to extensive use of aid – a slow and laborious process at the best of times, doubly so when soloing and pack hauling. Eventually the weather forced her to hunker down on a tiny ledge for four frustrating and extremely cold days.

The other thing that plagued her was the media circus – news of her climb had leaked out to the ever-hungry press (critics unfairly accused her of deliberately letting this happen) and quite literally scores of helicopters buzzed around her as she climbed, a tiny figure against the huge expanse of golden granite. Some climbers criticized her use of a portaledge, which added quite a few kilograms to her load, and some 'hard-core' alpinists claimed that it made the route much easier. However, this piece of equipment justified its existence when she was forced to the spend four days hanging in space in the midst of a blizzard.

At one stage, in the middle of the route, a series of aid pieces ripped on a fragile expanding flake system, and Catherine took a 10m (33ft) fall. Although not seriously injured, she was badly shaken, and could not resume climbing for a good few hours. She graded the aid on this section A4+, making it some of the most demanding aid done in the Alps at that stage. Jeff Lowe's Metanoia (see p59) is to date the only climb to have aid at A5.

Eventually, after 10 days and 20 pitches, she arrived at the quartz ledges that make up the last section of the pillar. There she bivouacked for the last time, and the next day in fine weather made short work of the final overhangs and reached the top of the ridge, a diminutive figure in a vast landscape.

Ever a magnet for controversy, Catherine now did something she afterwards deeply regretted – one of the multitude of passing helicopters offered her a lift down, and she accepted. At that stage, she said, 'I was tired, and all I wanted was a hot bath!' By accepting the 'easy way out' she opened yet another window for her critics to fire into.

The normal descent, via abseil onto the Flammes de Pierre ridge, is in itself quite a tricky and epic adventure (although she had done this twice before). The idea of a long slog with her heavy gear could not have been an appealing one, and most felt that she had already justified her actions by opening the most difficult new route ever to be done by a woman.

'My position of being a kind of celebrity provokes jealousy and backbiting, but I try not to notice this...I live life passionately; there is great pleasure in this and that takes care of everything.' (Destivelle in 'Beyond Risk', *Conversations with Climbers*, Nicholas O'Connell)

Divine Providence – Mont Blanc

The right choice at the right time

MONT BLANC, THE HIGHEST POINT IN WESTERN Europe, is, as its name suggests, a beautiful cone of white snow and ice. It was ascended many years back, on 8 August 1786 (an interesting coincidence with Divine Providence), by Michel Gabriel Paccard and Jacques Balmat via the Aiguille de Goutier and Dome de Goutier route on the French side of the mountain.

There is no doubt that Mont Blanc and its many satellite peaks are the 'heart of alpinism'. Countless climbers head for the ice, snow, rock and mixed routes which adorn the slopes of Mont Blanc itself, and also the hundreds of ridges and fine rock towers (*aiguilles,* or needles) which surround it. Partly because of these large numbers, it claims many lives each year, perhaps not surprisingly mostly on the 'easy' routes where the Alpine traps of fickle weather, crevasses, avalanches and rockfall lie in wait for the unwary and underprepared.

To modern extreme climbers, the only major approaches worth considering are those from the much steeper Italian side, particularly the Brenva area. Here a number of superb ridges, faces and pillars lure climbers onto both established routes and to the ultimate prize – a new route up a previously unclimbed piece of the mountain. Legendary names such as Sentinelle Rouge, The Innominata, Central Pillar of Frêney, and Brenva Spur act like a magnet to the alpinist.

Mont Blanc is reckoned to have three great rock faces – the Brouillard Face, the Frêney Face, and the Grand Pilier d'Angle. All of these are 'modern' Alpine faces, with long and often dramatic histories. The Grand Pilier d'Angle (or Eckpfeiler) gained fame in 1957 when Walter Bonatti and Toni Gobbi (both Alpine heroes of the age) climbed the series of diagonal chimneys and cracks on the 'unclimbable' 750m (2460ft) East Face. This to some extent avoided the main difficulties, but this was rectified by the Bonatti-Zapelli route on the northeast face in 1962. This climb has great objective dangers – stonefall and icefall from the hanging glacier on the face as well as the unusually large top séracs – and the lower pitches are generally done in the very early hours of the morning. In 1971 Walter Cecchinel and Georges Nominé completed a stunning line just to the right of the Bonatti-Gobbi route that was regarded as the hardest on the face until Divine Providence came into being 13 years later. The Cecchinel-Nominé route, although technically difficult, soon moves out of the line of major icefall, and is thus a fairly safe and popular climb.

The route

In its day Divine Providence, a gruelling route, was by far the hardest climb leading to the summit of Mont Blanc, and it is still ranked as one of the hardest and most desirable. The giant Brenva Face

Route	
Divine Providence	
Grade	
ED3–4/A3/6a, free at ED4/5.7c	
Peak/Height	
Mont Blanc, 4808m (15,775ft)	
Area	
Brenva Face (Italian side), Mont Blanc, France	
Length	
900m (2950ft) to Peuterey Ridge	
Date of first ascent	
5–8 August 1984	
Climbers	
Patrick Gabarrou, François Marsigny (both of France)	

Opposite Irishman Brendon Murphy exiting from the red wall (the Shield) and heading for the Peuterey Ridge on day five, during his and New Zealander Dave Wills's ascent of Divine Providence.

looms over the Brenva Glacier, with the Pilier d'Angle standing at the point where the Peuterey Ridge steepens from the Col de Peuterey on its way to the Col Major and hence to the summit of Mont Blanc. The Pilier itself rises in a series of steep triangular steps of grey and red granite. The most significant feature is a huge tower of red rock situated above the set of cracks and chimneys which seem to focus themselves like arrows on the base of the tower. Significantly all of the routes until 1984 had avoided the Red Tower, skipping either left or right in the crack systems that criss-cross at the base of the looming mass of blank red rock. The obvious route was the *diretissima* through the tower itself, and it took climbers of the stature and boldness of Frenchmen Patrick Gabarrou and François Marsigny to achieve this.

The route starts at the lowest point of the Pilier d'Angle, and commences on a huge ramp which rises at a slight leftwards slope for 400m (1300ft) (mostly grades IV and V with a few harder moves) to cross the Bonatti-Gobbi chimneys at the very base of the Red Tower. The real *diretissima* starts here, with a set of wide cracks leading onto the 350m-high (1150ft) tower (Grade V to VII+, with A2/A3 moves in its original form). The route then joins the Bonatti-Gobbi East Face route for the final 150m (500ft) to the Peuterey Ridge, and via this to the summit of Mont Blanc.

The climbers

Patrick Gabarrou is a prolific Alpine climber. What Bonatti was to the Alps in the late 1950s and early 1960s, Gabarrou was to them in the 1980s. A number of excellent routes throughout the Mont Blanc range, in particular, bear his name, although the Lyskamm, Breithorn and the huge Nordend all sport his superb quality climbs.

François Marsigny is equally an Alpine fundi, with a good deal of experience in soloing routes. In 1993 he was unceremoniously hauled off the Petit Dru on the first winter solo attempt of

the French *diretissima*, having spent eight days on the face. However, he regained his pride with numerous fine climbs after that.

The climb

August is reckoned as the ideal month for summer climbing in the Alps. The weather is mild to warm and generally at its most stable, and much of the accumulated ice and snow from the previous winter has been swept or melted off the faces and the tops. The rock is as dry as it is likely to get. This is the season when the cutting edge routes get established. 1984 had been a good season. The weather had settled into a pattern which gave a few clear days, then a summer storm, with fairly predictable

regularity. Gabarrou had been eyeing the line of Divine Providence for some years, and had taken a closer look in 1983 when he did the Gabarrou-Long route just left of the Cecchinel-Nominé, up the right-hand edge of the Pilier (at IV to IV+ not too hard, but still not a route to be trifled with). Marsigny was available, and the pair headed off in the crisp, clear cold long before daybreak over familiar glacier territory to the base of the actual rock. The long ramp was easily disposed of, despite

Top left Dave Wills (New Zealand) leading up the overhanging dihedral on the third day of a repeat of Divine Providence.

Bottom left A heavily laden Brendan Murphy, from Ireland, leading the hard roof pitch on day four.

Above right Brendan Murphy enjoying the only decent ledge on the route after the efforts of day three.

Opposite Moving up onto easier ground on the last day, the Brenva Glacier visible far below. The climb is not over yet, as the Peuterey Ridge and the summit of Mont Blanc with it's accompanying descent still lie ahead of the climbers.

being consistent Grade IV and V. The first pitches of the tower, large Grade V chimneys with poor protection, were climbed and ropes fixed, then the pair retreated to a tiny bivouac ledge at the base.

The next morning the climbing started in earnest. The face offered little by way of continuous cracks, and a good deal of hunting around was necessary. Immaculate thin cracks gave hard aid pitches on tiny RPs (brass wedges the size of a matchhead) and pegs which did not go in too deeply. A few times pieces 'popped' out, and the leader would fly downwards until the rope and a slightly more solid placement held him. The climb was a tense affair for climber and belayer alike. A series of small overhangs and one large roof at Grade VII brought the pair to the next resting spot, a hanging bivouac at the base of what proved to be the most time-consuming pitch,

the crux open-book corner. This long thin crack between two nearly featureless faces yielded slowly. Aid was inevitable, and the pitch eventually went at VII+/A3, after virtually a full day of climbing. This pitch had very sparse protection widely spaced up the long, overhanging crack.

Then the climbing eased off and Peuterey Ridge was reached via a small snowfield. A few hours on the fine, classic ridge, and Mont Blanc de Courmayeur and Mont Blanc itself soon appeared to the weary pair.

Divine Providence, recognized as the test piece for extreme alpinists, has seen a large number of attempts, and quite a few successful repeats. It was soloed by Frenchman Christophe Lafaille on 4–5 August 1990, and climbed almost entirely free by Thierry Renault and Alain Ghersen in the same

season, with the sixth pitch on the Red Wall now forming the crux at 7C. Italians Occi, Tamagini and Bressan made the first winter ascent of the route, but did not go to the summit of Mont Blanc. Brendan Murphy (Ireland) and Dave Wills (New Zealand) made the first winter ascent of the route to the summit of Mont Blanc in December 1992 (spending Christmas day on the face) at ED2–3/ A3/F6b. Alain Ghersen made the first winter solo in 1993, but placed a bolt on Red Tower's 7a+ or A3 pitch – perhaps an unfortunate move for someone who had already done the route without the need for the security of a bolt placement.

Divine Providence will undoubtedly tempt the extreme climber for many years until it enters into the realm of classic routes and more modern extreme routes replace it as the *pièce de résistance*.

The Gift – Rockies

A gift that keeps on giving

THE ALASKAN ROCKIES ARE A WILD AND beautiful range of mountains which contain Mt McKinley (Denali), at 6194m (20,332ft) the highest peak in North America. The climbing on most of the peaks is truly expeditionary in nature, as they are remote in terms of access, and weather conditions are changeable and semi-arctic. At a latitude of 60 degrees or so north, these are some of the coldest mountain regions outside of Antarctica, adding to the challenge for the climber. An interesting phenomenon is the 'barometric dip' experienced close to the poles, where centripetal and climatic forces act to lower air pressure by up to 10 percent. The effect is to 'raise the altitude' of the peaks in climbing terms, making a 6000m (19,700ft) peak roughly equivalent to close to 7000m (23,000ft). The plus side to the high latitudes is the long days in summer – balanced, of course, by the endless nights in winter.

The routes all have dangers of crevasses, avalanches and ice falls, putting them further in line with the Himalayan giants. Despite this, the peaks see a good deal of traffic each year, in particular Denali. The outlying peaks are wilder and more isolated, and give climbers a sense of commitment and adventure. Mt Bradley, only a few kilometres from Denali, experiences not even two percent of the number of climbers – who usually only do the standard ridges and North Face, despite it offering many exceptional climbs.

The peak

Mt Bradley lies on the eastern side of the Alaskan range, which rises suddenly and dramatically from the plains below. This causes it to experience both low temperatures and sudden weather changes. These same rapid changes are responsible for the many lives lost on Denali and its satellite peaks each year. Although considerably lower than Denali, the steepness of Mt Bradley's faces and the amount of climbable rock have led to an increasing number of expeditions in the past few years. The giant South Face is characterized by a number of pillars, which give outstanding climbing on solid granite. The most dramatic route on Bradley's faces is The Pearl, put up by Andy Orgler, solo, on the central pillar. Mt Bradley is separated from the massif of Denali by the complex, multiforked Ruth Glacier. Some of the most difficult climbs in the Denali massif lie above here, among them the Isis Ridge and the Ridge of No Return, which were climbed by Renato Casarotto, solo, in 1985.

The route

The South Face of Mt Bradley sweeps around in a huge amphitheatre, split on the west by two angled couloirs that lead onto an ice bowl. The eastern side of this amphitheatre is dominated by the 1100m (3600ft) South Pillar, which towers skywards in an almost unbroken mass of granite. A large, slightly

Route
The Gift that Keeps on Giving

Grade
5.9/A3/WI6

Peak/Height
South Pillar, Mt Bradley, 1100m (3609ft)

Area
Alaskan Rockies, USA

Length
975m (3200ft)

Date of first ascent
March 1999

Climbers
Mark Twight, Steve House, Jonny Blitz (all of the USA)

Opposite American Steve House leads up the imposing gully halfway up The Gift That Keeps on Giving – the demanding mixed nature of the route can be seen in the loosely adhering ice and the overhanging rock.

broken gully system bounds the pillar on the west, and The Gift follows this gully. It is a 960m (3150ft) route that was completed in 23 pitches, most of which were a full rope length (60m; 200ft). The easier, lower approach pitches were climbed unroped, but that might not be the method subsequent ascensionists would prefer.

The climbers

Mark Twight (USA) has been an activist in pushing the frontiers of mixed and big-wall climbing over the past decade. He is perhaps best known for his Great and Secret Show in Baffin Island, although his experience stretches from hard climbs in Canada (Ice Palace, Reality Bath) and Alaska to South America and the Himalaya. He was recently elected to the prestigious Groupe de la Haute Montagne.

Steve House has been at the forefront of American ice and mixed climbing for a long time. He completed a 36-hour first ascent of the Fathers and Sons Wall on Denali, and a new route on the 1850m (6069ft) West Face.

Fellow American Jonny Blitz came back from a nine-year break to tackle The Gift; however he had previously climbed a good deal with Mark Twight, and he is a very accomplished all-rounder.

The climb

The year 1999 had seen a particularly wet season in Alaska, which had the boon of creating more solid than usual waterfall ice, the downside of which was more snow to fall off tops and ridges, and more hidden crevasses. With El Niño creating mild weather, many climbers established climbs in areas they had been eyeing for a while before the 'great thaw' dumped the snow down on the routes.

The trio flew out to the base camp on the Ruth Glacier on 28 February – quite early in the season – in order to utilize the already moderately long days while the ice was still solidly frozen. They were not as yet set on a line, but wanted to look at what was on offer, as route conditions can vary from season to season. After a few days of ski-tour examination, the line of The Gift appeared the most appealing.

The first attempt at the line ended in retreat after pitch 5. The ice low down was not as good as had been hoped, with the first real roped pitch consisting of no more than soft frothy snow thinly plastered on rock. Pitch 2 had to be climbed with

crampons scrabbling on the rock on the side of the ice. Pitch 3 went rapidly only after a long lead-out without any gear placed suddenly ended at the full 60m (196ft), with no anchors of any worth available. Blitz eventually ended up giving his partners a tenuous belay off shallowly placed ice tools. House then tackled pitch 4, but eventually had to take his pack off and hang it on one of the few ice screws he managed to place so that he could manage the balancey, technical climbing on thin, insecure ice. At this point the group, after eyeing the hair-raising 6th pitch, decided to opt out while they still had some daylight left, and abseiled off.

Opposite Steve House following pitch 10 on water ice, thinly plastered over friable rock. 'This is the challenge that keeps us going, folks!' The route was characterized by fragile ice that splintered off at the first attempt to use it, making for nerve-wracking climbing.

Above Superb front-pointing on thin but good ice as House moves into the large gully system on pitch 11. The meaningfully named 'Hateful Wall' pitch that caused so much hardship and toil looms above.

Right A cold but patient Mark Twight watching House's manoeuvres above him. The tangle of gear and ropes all had to be hauled up pitch by pitch, an extremely energy-draining process.

On 7 March they were back, and made rapid progress over their previous ground. Pitch 6 (called The Super Third Eye Opener because of its committing nature) was not as difficult as expected, but still dangerous, with loose ice and scant protection. This pitch was the key to escaping from the small, blind gully into the major chimney, in which they put up another three pitches before calling it a day. The next day saw pleasant climbing up to The Super Giant Waterfall of Love pitch, led by House. This was at first climbed on deep, unconsolidated snow onto good mixed climbing, then a huge icicle above a cave. House pulled up on this, which snapped off above his axe placements, giving him a rodeo ride onto the snow slope during which his first piece of gear pulled out. Fortunately the second, a camming device, held, and stopped his fall. After a brief recovery he headed back onto the icicle, which fortunately allowed him to climb it onto a steep thin pillar and thence via an unprotected ramp to a chockstone belay. This pitch took two and a half hours of sustained, nerve-wracking effort.

On the third day, they decided that the difficulty of the climbing warranted leaving large packs behind – either they would reach the top, or abseil back to the bivvy gear. Pitch 15 turned out to be an A3 horror that took as many hours as its grade. This pitch was led using ice axes to aid off, with the odd tied-off knifeblade, some bulldog ice hooks and a lot of to-ing and fro-ing to collect equipment for re-use as their leading rack was not large enough for this sort of extended aid climbing. The obvious consequence of this re-use of gear was the elimination of protection points, making the pitch doubly dangerous.

After this, the climb moved into an easier gully, which went free up to another huge chockstone. This was turned on the right in two hard pitches of mixed climbing, with rock and small sections of ice alternating. Darkness was falling as they bumped into yet another giant chockstone, but some digging and 'constructive ice modification' allowed them to climb behind it, onto a 90-degree waterfall pitch.

At 20:00 they reached the col above the gully, at 2677m (8783ft). The true summit lay well back and 125m (410ft) away, on easy snow. The decision was made to 'leave the summit' and the group rappelled off, reaching the bivvy ledge at 01:30. The next day they abseiled down the route, cleaning whatever gear they could from the rock and ice.

The Gift that Keeps on Giving represents one of the longest and most serious mixed routes opened in North America. The climb was done in subzero temperatures which necessitated wearing gloves, even on pure rock pitches. Half of the 26 pitches were 'hard', either at Grade 5.9 rock, or VI ice, with the added difficulties of climbing on aid with crampons and boots to Grade A3. Throughout the entire climb protection was minimal and a fall would have been extremely serious, if not tragic.

Opposite top Jonny Blitz leading, with Steve House in a hanging belay on pitch 12. The route continues up the loose and dangerous vertical gulley system beyond.
Opposite bottom An unusually comfortable bivouac, the spacious Super Shroom, above pitch 12. 'Are you warm enough, matey?' This ledge gave the team a much-needed respite from hanging bivouacs.
Right The Super Three-hour Pitch, number 15. This involved delicate A3 work on hooks – not an easy task at this altitude, particularly in gloves and crampons. The precariously poised Jonny Blitz looks uncertain that the étriers will stay put!

Big Wall Climbs

El Niño. Ship of Fools. Grand Voyage. Riders on the Storm. Slovenian Route. Moby Dick. Midgard Serpent.

THE CONCEPT OF A 'BIG WALL' IN CLIMBING terms is somewhat of a problem as it means different things to different people. To some it means the pure rock faces of Yosemite, to others a distant expanse of rock, ice and snow in the Himalayas. Most climbers would understand it to mean a huge mountain face where the climbing takes place over a number of days, primarily on rock although ice and snow may feature. This concept has altered over time, and big-wall techniques are now being applied to routes of alpine or Himalayan scale. Modern 'speed climbing' ascents have also redefined time boundaries, with many once-multiday routes now being ascended in a matter of hours.

Big-wall climbing got its name and impetus in the Yosemite Valley, where climbers such as Royal Robbins and Warren Harding put time-warp routes up the 30- to 50-pitch, 1000m (3281ft), smooth granite walls in the early 1960s. These routes involved long sections of free climbing, but also relied heavily on aiding – standing or pulling on the gear (largely pitons, at that stage). In conventional big-wall climbing the face was 'sieged', that is, in order to save time, some of the climbers jumared up pitches after the leader. Food, bivouac gear and other equipment was progressively hauled up in sacks or bags.

At the same time, the European climbers were working on the massive dolomite walls such as those of the Tre Címe di Laveredo, as well as in the central Alps, such as the Aiguille du Blaitier and the Petit Dru. The 'new' discovery was the Norwegian Troll wall (1500m; 5000ft high), which gave a host of impressive routes. It was first climbed in 1965 by Tony Howard, Bill Tweedale and John Amatt via the Rimmon route, now largely missing as a result of a huge rockfall a short while ago. Plenty of new-routing for the bold to do...

In the early 1970s, Baffin Island (the Canadian Rockies), caught the eye of climbers via a newly issued set of the photographs taken by Pat Baird in his 1953 expedition. The stunning granite pillars began to receive their (over)due attention.

Ship of Fools, Grand Voyage, Riders on the Storm, Moby Dick and the Slovenian Route on Cerro Torre are all extreme climbs on huge and remote expanses of rock, done in the face of icefall, avalanches, and at the mercy of fickle weather.

El Niño represents a current trend in places such as Yosemite – it uses sections of existing routes, with short original linking passages, but has been given its own name as it has been climbed free – without resorting to aid; it is thus considered a 'new' route (it is a free rock climb on a big wall). Pack-hauling is still used, but in the first ascent both climbers climbed all the pitches.

Climbing massive mountain faces and walls at altitude is the logical progression. The distinction between Big Walls and Big Mountains is increasingly being eroded. Spantik's Golden Pillar route (see pp135–137) could for instance just as well have been placed in the big wall section, although the approach was more capsule style (see p129).

Jason Smith's solo ascent of Midgard Serpent on Mt Thor, one of the largest walls in the world, illustrates another trend in big-walling; lonely repeats of desperately hard climbs.

Previous pages Kevin Thaw contemplating life from his bat tent on The Shortest Straw, Yosemite.
Opposite, left to right A flake and granite crystal provide strenuous but welcome leverage on Moby Dick, southern Greenland; the vast array of protection gear in the foreground is of little use in this awkward, off-width crack on Riders on the Storm, Patagonia, South America; the belayer getting things organized on El Niño in the Yosemite Valley.
Right Bongard and Middendorf on the elegant flutes and stalactites on the final rock pitches of the Grand Voyage.

El Niño – El Capitan

A climb to shake North America

THE YOSEMITE VALLEY IS ONE OF THE legendary climbing areas. Deep in the heart of a national park, it is a superbly beautiful glacial valley, with walls of immaculate granite rising to 1000m (3280ft) from the valley floor. The Valley is dominated by two main features – Half Dome, and the bulk of El Capitan.

The 'right' side (the southeast face) of El Cap, known as the North America Wall because of the shape of a set of dolerite dykes through which the climb North America Wall passes, is reputed to be one of the blankest and most difficult Yosemite walls.

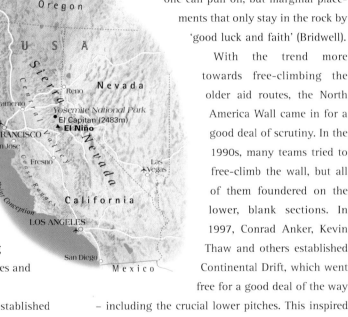

In 1975, Pacific Ocean Wall was established by Jim Bridwell and team, just to the left of North America Wall. This route has pitches of A4, including many copperhead placements (copperheads are tiny soft brass 'nuts' which get 'mashed' into cracks which are too shallow to accept standard nuts, pitons or camming devices; they are body-weight-only devices and of little use in stopping a fall).

In 1978, Jim Bridwell and partners established Sea of Dreams, an A5 route which cuts through North America Wall at about two-thirds' height. This route has seven compulsory pendulums, and a good deal of 'hooking' (the aid climber stands on a tiny metal 'hook', which just holds in a crack under his weight). The gear used included 75 pitons, 35 camming units, 100 copperheads, and a large variety of sizes and shapes of hooks. Not a route for the faint-hearted.

All of these routes demand a great deal from the climbers – a cool head, boldness, innovation and tremendous determination. The climbers are frequently way above any decent protection, relying on their strength and tenacity to get them through the 'vast unknown' until they (hopefully) reach a serviceable protection point. Long falls are common, many of them verging on the limits of what the rope, the protection and the belay system will hold. At grades of A4 and A5, the aid is no longer just good, comfortable stuff that one can pull on, but marginal placements that only stay in the rock by 'good luck and faith' (Bridwell).

With the trend more towards free-climbing the older aid routes, the North America Wall came in for a good deal of scrutiny. In the 1990s, many teams tried to free-climb the wall, but all of them foundered on the lower, blank sections. In 1997, Conrad Anker, Kevin Thaw and others established Continental Drift, which went free for a good deal of the way – including the crucial lower pitches. This inspired the efforts that went into El Niño.

The climbers

The brothers Alexander and Thomas Huber from Germany have established quite a reputation over the past two decades. Despite being siblings, and frequently climbing with one another from their earliest days in the town of Berchtesgaden, they started in their late twenties to concentrate on

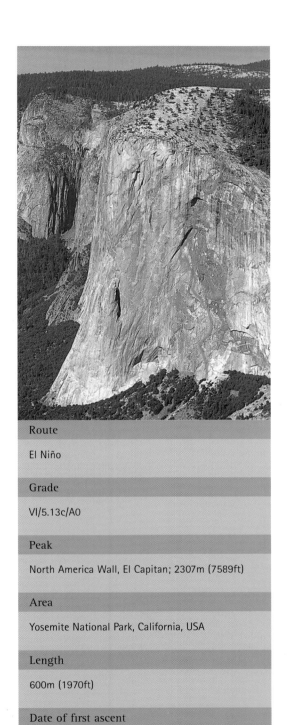

Route	
El Niño	
Grade	
VI/5.13c/A0	
Peak	
North America Wall, El Capitan; 2307m (7589ft)	
Area	
Yosemite National Park, California, USA	
Length	
600m (1970ft)	
Date of first ascent	
September 1998	
Climbers	
Alexander and Thomas Huber (Germany)	

Opposite Dawn light on the imposing bulk of El Capitan, forging ground of big-wall climbing. The Nose route follows the central line of light and shadow; El Niño moves through the dark patches on the extreme right-hand face.

differing climbing arenas. Thomas, the older by two years, laid more emphasis on the Alpine arena, and gained his reputation in the Wendenstock and Berchtesgaden Alps, with cutting-edge routes such as Scaramouche (IX+/X-), and The End of Silence (XI-) done with Alex.

Alex tended more towards the sport and crag climbing, and his achievements include the hardest of sport routes such as Black Power (8C+) and Weisse Rose (8C+) in Schleierwasserfall in 1994, and of course the 1996 Open Air (9a).

With his free ascent of the Salathé route on El Cap in 1995 at 5.13b, Alex leapt to the forefront of climbing. As he put it: 'To be "state of the art" in sport climbing for years is very hard work for your mind as well as your body. After years of consistent training, it is difficult to maintain motivation for goals that are more or less repetitions of things you have already achieved. Such feelings are poisonous to a climber's motivation. Thus, after ten years of climbing and mountaineering in the Alps, I found myself searching for a new way – a search that in 1995 led me out of Europe for the first time.' Salathé was the result.

The search continued with the ascent of Latok II via the impressive West Face ('El Cap on top of Denali', as it has been described), together with Thomas. Thereafter came Cho Oyu, Alex's first 8000m (26,000ft) peak. Four months later, he was standing in Yosemite with Thomas, eyeing the North America Wall.

The climb

The pair started off from the Footstool, a distinctive 50m (160ft) pillar leaning against the face 'like a lost island'. They climbed the first pitches, the section between Wyoming Sheep Ranch (VI/A5+) and Gulf Stream (VI/5.9/A4). They moved onto the Continental Drift Black Dike sections, and thence (at 5.13b) to the Missing Link traverse and the dramatic 5.13c Galapagos pitches – delicate but strenuous traversing on marginal protection. Once again, one must not imagine that it is all plain

sailing, and that falls are not serious. The Hubers refused to be lulled into placing extra, solid bolts into the existing route. They relied on what they found or what natural gear they could place. The running belays (the protection points) and the belay stances themselves were as tenuous as any which the aid climbers used. In many cases, the consequences of a fall – more likely on the free ascent than on the aid ascent – could have been serious, if not fatal. The climbers were constantly on edge, both mentally and physically, fully aware that there was no room for error. 'Easier' (5.11d) climbing led to the eventual Big Sur bivouac – 'the best on the face', according to Alex.

The essence of free-climbing a route such as the North America Wall is that the climbers may not pull on, stand on, or use aid in any way. Pendulums and tension traverses are no exceptions to the rule – where previous ascensionists have pendulumed, the 'free' ascensionists must cross the barrier under their own steam.

From the Big Sur ledge to the next crack system, the aptly named Royal Arches, lay three pendulum pitches. The first was attained at 5.13a, but the next led to 3m (10ft) of blank, impassable granite. Ray Jardine, on his first free ascent of

Opposite left to right Negotiating one of the pitches adjacent to the Cyclop's Eye, North America Wall; a more than well-equipped climber on Lost in America; Andre Vancampenhoud cleaning a traverse on the North America Wall.
Above right Taking a break on a midway bivouac ledge, El Capitan. Rehydration is a constant necessity, and water usually forms the largest portion of the haul bag's weight. Part of the vast array of gear needed is seen in the foreground.

The Nose of El Capitan solved a similar problem by chopping small holds into the blank granite – the Jardine Traverse. However, the brothers looked for another solution and found it in their now notorious Man-powered Rappel. Eight metres (26ft) below and left of their tiny stance was a hands-off rest on the Endurance Corner pitch. If the climber could get there, he was able to free-climb onwards. The obvious solution was to rappel (abseil) there, but this would break the rules. To solve this and avoid the situation where either climber hangs on protection, the belayer hangs on his fingertips from the belay ledge with his ropes slack to the protection points, i.e. no loading of the ropes, while the climber down-climbs. After a metre or two, the climber's weight comes onto a rope tied to the belayer's harness – a short 4m (13ft) rappel on this rope brings the climber to a ledge, where he can take weight off the belayer for a few seconds, then a second 4m (13ft) rappel brings him to the belay at the next no-hands rest. In one of the brother's words: 'Of course the Man-powered Rappel cannot be referred to as having been redpointed, but it follows the guidelines for free-climbing: movement over rock using just the natural surface. It was an acceptable solution for us.' This it might have been, but to many other climbers, it would be terrifying.

Once this barrier had been crossed, the rest of the route went relatively easily, with the exception of one pitch. The Black Dihedral led to the Black Cave, where a scary and sustained set of roof moves at 5.13b were protected only by a single, old, sawn-off angle piton. The climber moves metres out into yawning space, with the face overhanging below. Any fall would leave the leader dangling way out in space from a suspect piece of gear, with return to the wall extremely difficult.

The pair then climbed the rest of the route via a set of pitches with evocative names such as The Cyclop's Eye, The Eismeer, The Igloo and the North Pole (the final, 30th pitch). Their initial exploration of the route was over; all of the moves had been worked out.

From this initial foray to determine the pathway and feasibility of the climb came the redpoint attempt – to succeed, both brothers had to free-climb all 30 pitches without falling, aiding or resting on gear. After a few days of rest in the Valley, this was achieved in three hard days of climbing, giving El Cap the route El Niño, VI/5.13c/A0 – a spectacular combination of new pitches with sections of older routes such as New Jersey Turnpike, Continental Drift, Heavy Metal and Tinker Toys, Sea of Dreams, and of course, North America Wall itself.

The second ascent

Although this book essentially covers only first ascents of routes, the second ascent of El Niño came so soon after the first, and in such an unusual fashion, that it deserves mention. Wunderkinder are no new thing to climbing – it took the likes of youngsters such as Joe Brown and Don Whillans, Layton Kor, Pat Ament, Gaston Rebuffet, Johnny Dawes and Ben Moon, to name but a few, to put older climbers to shame or simply to raise standards by 'doing their own thing'.

While the 'elderly' (30-ish) Hubers were forging El Niño, two young (very young) British climbers were heading for the valley. As Alex went for Free Rider, the second (variation) free ascent of Salathé *and* first solo – to follow the El Niño success (later he and Thomas speed-climbed it in 15 hours), Leo Houlding and Patch Hammond were lying soaking up the sun (and beer) and watching the German pair at play. Their decision was made: 'We want to do El Niño free, fast, and on-sight.' The philosophy of the pair (who had never actually even seen a big wall before this first visit to Yosemite) was simple: 'Big-walling is easy. We'll take climbing gear, camping gear (of vertical context) and "shitloads" of water.'

The highly big-wall-inexperienced pair set off, and proceeded to fly up the route, following the generously given Huber brothers' topo (and also later making use of pieces of tape the Hubers had stuck onto the rock here and there on which they marked the type of protection for that point; their way of saving time and energy on the redpoint ascent – perhaps a dubious ethic). The route was sadly not a total, clean, on-sight – Leo grabbed a quickdraw on the first (5.13b) pitch to avoid a 20m (65ft) fall, resulting from his overconfidence on the initial technical, balance moves. However, all of the rest of the pitches were climbed clean, on-sight – including the two 5.13c pitches – an amazing feat anywhere, let alone on a wall of the scale of Yosemite!

Leo Houlding had, of course, as a 17-year-old, gained a subsequently justified reputation with his on-sight ascent of the famed and ill-protected Master's Wall in Wales – the second successful attempt ever, despite many tries by the cream of the climbing crop. Incredible skill combined with extreme boldness has become the hallmark of this

impetuous yet pleasant young climber, often paired with the equally young and like-talented (but possibly more cautious) Patrick (Patch) Hammond. The pair got caught by the first fierce Yosemite storm of the season, lost their way on a few key pitches, and eventually topped out in inky darkness and snow at the end of their second day, tired but ecstatic. Houlding likened the loose rock of the black

sections to 'being like Gogarth' – a British crag notorious for loose rock and looser language. In the words of Leo, 'El Niño was my first Big Wall. The feeling of exposure, excitement, partnership and fun, combined with the experiences of a big wall, dominate my memories of the climb. The best route I have ever done. Thirty-three star routes in one!'

Opposite Don't spill! The concentration on the climber's face reveals the difficulties and challenges of cooking on an unstable portaledge high above ground.
Above left Tim Wagner jumaring up Sea of Dreams – the piton hammer will soon come into use to remove the single peg which he is totally dependent on.
Above right A bolt belay gives Sue Nott some semblance of security before a typical Yosemite peg traverse.

Ship of Fools – Shipton Spire

Climbing under the guillotine

THE BALTORO GLACIER, IN THE GREATER Karakorum mountain range, flows east–west. Three 8000m (26,000ft) giants, K2, Broad Peak and Gasherbrum cluster around its head, while the incredible rock towers that attract so many climbers rise just to the north. The Latok group lies northwest, above the Biafo Glacier. The Trango Glacier leads off northwards past the Trango Towers on the east (see p105) and Uli Biaho and Paiju on the west. Trango Glacier is lined with countless rock spires, one of which cannot be seen unless one moves up a side glacier towards Choricho (6756m; 22,166ft) – a beautiful tooth of pure rock, Shipton Spire.

In 1930, Eric Shipton, the indefatigable British explorer, travelled up the Trango Glacier and took photographs which clearly showed the then-unnamed spire. It was only in 1989 that Greg Collum, an American climber, saw the pictures, and took a group in that direction from the well-known and populous Trango base camp. A brief two hours later, the huge 1400m (4600ft) of flawless granite hove into view. Greg named it the Shipton Spire, as a tribute to the man who first saw it.

The peak

After investigating the Spire in 1989, Collum began to plan an assault. He was back in 1992 with a strong team, who fought the rigours of the cold, weather, and falling ice and rock to forge a route up the southwest ridge, but sadly had to turn back a scant 250m (820ft) from the summit in the face of bad weather and lack of food. The subsequent report in *Climbing* magazine brought a flush of interest in this undiscovered gem, including the 1995 attempt by a young Japanese, Ryuchi Taniguchi. He was halfway up on this same route when a rockfall ripped him from the wall. His body was eventually found and removed, but his tattered haul bags still remain as a grim monument to the power of the peak.

In 1996, Greg Collum returned, with Chuck Boyd from his original team, and powerful additions in Greg Child and Greg Foweraker. They chose a long route on the central pillar of the south face. Collum retreated about halfway, partly due to the inherent danger of the chosen route, mostly due to tensions in the group. The other three continued fighting (in more ways than one, it would appear) their way up the 36-pitch route, and reached the final 14m (45ft) of unconsolidated snow. At this point they decided that 'enough was enough' and descended, claiming the first ascent of this indisputably major peak.

The result of this claim was a wild and irrational media frenzy about 'summitless first ascents', including editorial articles in the respected *American Alpine Journal* and *Climbing* magazine. Kennedy, the editor of *Climbing*, likened their ascent to others in Alaska and the Yukon that had ended hundreds of feet from the summit – perhaps

Route	
Ship of Fools	
Grade	
VII/5.11/A2/WI6	
Peak/Height	
Shipton Spire, 6004m (19,700ft)	
Area	
Central Karakorum, Pakistan	
Length	
1350m (4400ft)	
Date of first ascent	
August 1997	
Climbers	
Mark Synnott, Jared Ogden (both USA)	

Opposite An unusually relaxed climber making the most of excellent weather while scouting the face of Shipton Spire. Days such as this are rare in the Karakorum and the warm clothing scattered around will, no doubt, soon come in handy.

an unfair comparison. In 1997 in *Climbing* Greg Child made the point that Briton Joe Brown and George Band had stopped a few feet off the 8677m (28,521ft) summit of Kangchenjunga in respect of the Buddhist tradition; similarly, the summit of Nuptse (8954m; 29,378ft), in the middle of a long cornice, is seldom trodden. Child summed it up in his closing paragraphs:

'The experience has a tantalizing Zen quality to it: four puny humans on a virtually unknown peak overcome every obstacle of their climb except for a trivial mound of snow that would melt in a month. What could better express the delicious futility of climbing ... perhaps Shipton Spire taught us this: you can get so close to a summit that you can see on top of it, but in life we seldom get what we truly desire. Instead, we must be satisfied with the beauty of what we can hold in our hands.'

Of the three current routes on the Shipton Spire – The Baltese Falcon, Ship of Fools, and Inshallah – all would qualify as extreme. The choice of Ship of Fools is largely because it is the first truly undisputed ascent, it was done in great style by a two-man team, and it covered incredibly hard mixed ground.

The route

The route follows one of the many long crack lines on the North Face, more to the northeast of the aborted 1992 attempt. The first section consists of 800m (2600ft) of vertical wall, with good placements for aid and free-climbing gear. The route then moves onto a ridge, which slopes diagonally up rightwards, to join a rib, which has mixed

Above right After fresh snowfall, luxurious Camp 4 lies invitingly at the 'notch' around 5625m (18,455ft), in sharp contrast to the hanging bivouacs that characterize the remainder of the route.

Right Mark Synnott making the most of one of the all-too-frequent rainy days by hauling gear up the route.

Far right Jared Ogden nailing vertical seams low down on the route, the only significant aid of the climb, which was done approximately 80 percent free.

Opposite Ogden coming up the difficult, snow-covered, rising traverse on the ridge during the eight-day storm. His array of protection is not as solid as one would like.

climb again in four weeks. Jared himself had fractured his back in an avalanche a few months before, so the pair was not in great shape. 'Yet there was hope, for we wanted this climb more than we wanted functioning bodies. We were not going to take no for an answer.' (Ogden, *American Alpine Journal* 1998.) They left for the wall anyway.

The pair finally departed for their ride up the infamous Karakorum Highway, with 'drivers who were strung out on heroin'. Washed-away bridges and bartering officials were eventually left behind, and the 80km (50-mile) hike to base camp was underway. The camp was a pleasure – huge grassy meadows with unpolluted trickling streams and roaming ibex to keep them company.

Two days of load shuttling to advance base camp below the Spire followed, with the added insult of a totally incompetent base camp cook to greet them on their return. In the tradition of *Rum Doodle*, the classic parody on John Hunt's Everest book, the pair lived at advance base camp to escape the horrors of the cooking.

Each trip up the glacier, dodging crevasses and towering séracs, Synnott said 'it felt like we were trespassing into a forbidden zone'. Eventually they started off on the climbing proper, on what proved initially to be the fearsome rotten, crumbling granite they had been warned about. 'In some spots, it was like climbing under a guillotine' (Synnott, *Climbing*, March 1999). After three days they had fixed only 200m (650ft) of rope, and found a suitable site for the first bivvy. A number of days of rain followed their establishment on this ledge, leading to a wet and sodden few nights in inadequate bivvy bags. By this stage the bombardment of chunks of ice and rock was underway, and the grim remains of Taniguchi's haul bag brought no comfort. 'A sharp cracking sound resonated from above: we could hear something gathering speed. Something that sounded like a jumbo jet on its way down, creating a great wind disturbance as it thundered along. Tied to the ledge, Mark and I had nowhere to hide. There we were, a mere 200m [650ft] off the ground, and who knew how far this monster had fallen. Then it happened. A thousand pieces exploded all around. The biggest one destroyed the ledge we had belayed from one pitch below: a tombstone lay embedded in the ice. We looked out to inspect the damage – we were looking at a long wet night with new gashes in

climbing and steep ice leading to the summit. In essence, it is a straightforward-looking line, which hides a number of serious objective dangers.

The climbers

Mark Synnott (USA) has climbed more than 50 big walls including desperate first ascents such as The Great and Secret Show on the Polar Sun Spire, Great Trango and Cerro Torre. He holds the speed record for Yosemite's Lost in America. He is an accomplished ice climber, and a recognized author. Jared Ogden is firstly an ice climber – he hails from 'ice territory', Telluride in Colorado – secondly a rock climber, and thirdly a big wall man. The latter is belied by his ascent of The Book of Shadows, a most serious route on the Nameless Tower, and his routes on Mt Washington. He is known for his commitment to sketchy mixed climbs.

The climb

Just before leaving the USA, Mark called Jared with the news that he had just broken his ankle during his speed ascent of Lost in America on El Capitan, Yosemite; the doctor had assured him he would

our rain flysheet.' They decided to retire to base camp until the storm subsided, which it did the next day. 'On a big alpine wall climb, you walk a fine line between danger and safety, survival and fun. It was a test of our determination to jumar back up and commit to the wall. We pulled our five ropes up behind us, and never looked back.'

Soon they were at 5290m (17,365ft), on a large ledge at about the halfway mark nicknamed Fantasy Island. The rotten granite had long since given way to the compact, golden granite typical of the Karakorum. Their progress improved, as did the weather, and the climbing became 'glorious' – some superb 5.11 free-climbing – apart from the struggle to get enough oxygen into their straining lungs. The Slot From Hell pitch signalled the start of the next hard section – a crack that went from a pleasurable 100mm (4in) to an unclimbable body-absorbing size dreaded by climbers, then petered out until it was no more than a seam they had to bash copperheads in. The joy came in discovering at the top of this horrendous 80m (260ft) section a huge ledge on which they could even walk around.

As the climbing entered this new phase, described by Ogden as 'a blend of technical wizardry, savvy and hard free-climbing', so did the weather alter. Rain and snow began to fall about midday each day, and climbing from 05:00 to dark started to take its toll. Hands began to bleed from the constant cuts and abrasions brought on by the cold dry air and the necessity of climbing with numb, unfeeling fingers. By now everything was constantly wet, both inside and outside the tent, and subsequently frequently frozen solid, and this did not exclude the climbers. The daily grind of forcing their reluctant, damaged bodies to obey their perhaps equally reluctant minds displaced pleasure most of the time, replacing it with a grim, dogged determination to keep going.

The nature of the climbing now altered radically, from vertical and overhanging rock to a steep, knife-edged ridge of rock and ice 'like the dorsal fin of a prehistoric shark' (Synnott). Hard mixed climbing, switching from water ice to 5.9 rock with marginal protection on 600m (2000ft) of teetering ridge dropping off for thousands of feet on either side was no place to make mistakes. High winds and driving snow made progress slow and communication nigh impossible. Traversing proved almost more unnerving than vertical climbing, with both the leader and the second needing to be constantly on edge.

A series of towers breaking the knife-edge ridge caused great problems, as passing them on the sides with friable, loose rock and fragile ice was hazardous to the extreme, and going over them even more so. The final tower link-up was solved with a Tyrolean traverse – a wild ride down suspended ropes. Food supplies were dwindling. 'We began to dream about massive buffets and cookouts on the beach. It was time to finish the climbing.'

With only four power bars, 2 litres (3.5pt) of water and a minimum of gear left over, the summit bid was begun. The final face offered steep, fluted ice, with rock bands breaking the face at intervals for 200m (650ft). At last the overhanging cornice on the summit ridge came into view, just as the sun was disappearing. It would be a summit in the dark. In the confusion, Jared ended up jumaring an entire pitch tied only to Mark's harness – Mark had not had time to put in a belay, so he stood stoically in the waist-deep snow. Belay points were by now limited to a single insecure nut placement, with the climbing a mix of ice, 5.10 rock, and aid moves. 'Hanging from a single nut below an ice-smeared

chimney, I fed rope from the stack at my feet, rejoicing every time an inch went through my belay plate. I shouted encouragement to Jared until he pulled out of the chimney and his headlight disappeared.'

The final iced-up chimney was completed, and they were on the summit ridge, with the summit 30m (100ft) away. At 22:30, Mark reached the minute piece of rock that marked the summit, then down-climbed to allow Jared his turn. After a brief time on the summit, they realized that they had to return quickly to their bivouac ledge as they were starting to freeze. Thirteen abseils later, after battling frozen ropes that were more like steel cable than polyester, at 06:00 they finally made the tent on the large halfway ledge. Most rappels were off a single cam, nut, or a sling – a precarious undertaking, but one that saved on expensive gear. The following day they abseiled down the main wall, removing all of the gear they could, both of them

in a haze of exhaustion. 'The amount of work, determination and fun we had had on the Spire was almost over. As when watching your favourite movie over and over, I was reluctant for it to end.'

'We left our base camp as clean as we had found it. Our efforts, dreams and successes lay folded into the crevasses and fissures of Shipton Spire. Our presence may hardly be noticed, but we will never forget our ride on the Ship of Fools.'

As for the heated controversy that surrounds the first ascent? Take Mark Synnott's words as final judgement: 'Just remember the final 30ft [10m] of Shipton Spire was the only nontechnical section of a mountain with 4400ft (1340m) of vertical relief. I take my hat off to the climbers who laid the groundwork for our *second* ascent of Shipton Spire, and I say let's go back to the old system where climbers are *always* given the benefit of the doubt.'

Opposite Fantasy Island – the second bivvy on the climb. Careful management of gear is needed to ensure that vital items aren't inadvertently dropped. The route was climbed capsule-style – a major achievement on a wall this size.
Below left The long, exposed 15-pitch knife-edge which led to the tiny summit.
Below right Ogden leading difficult rock above nerve-wrackingly unconsolidated snow during the 24-hour summit push.

Grand Voyage – Great Trango

A trip into infinitely difficult territory

THE KARAKORUM RANGE GENERALLY HAS been described on p99. Its Baltoro region is a vast area, with the 58km-long (36-mile) Baltoro Glacier leading up to some of the world's highest peaks. The Trango Towers can be seen from the glacier as one treks to the top at Concordia, en route to K2, Broad Peak and the Gasherbrums.

The area is rugged, with little vegetation anywhere near the Trangos. It is a harsh and beautiful land of snow, rock and ice, of colossal granite walls and fickle weather. It is a mountaineer's paradise.

The Trango group consists of a number of peaks and towers, of which two reign supreme for the rock climber: that is, the Great Trango Tower (hereafter referred to as Great Trango), and the Nameless Tower (confusingly also called the Trango Tower). The Nameless Tower is quite possibly the largest pure 'rock needle' in the world, and as such has attracted many of the top names in climbing. Despite being smaller than Great Trango, the Nameless Tower's stunning pyramidal shape causes it to overshadow its big brother. The climbing history of the two towers is, however, interwoven, both having been the scene of epic climbs, descents, rescues and tragedies.

The Nameless Tower (so called by Galen Rowell, the great American climber and photographer) attracted the attention of legendary British 'hard man' Joe Brown, on his return from the ascent of

the Mustagh Tower in 1956. It was only in 1975, though, that he eventually returned to try it. The attempt failed just after a serious incident, sardonically described by Joe Brown as 'amusing', when Martin Boysen, way up above his nearest protection – a single bong lodged tenuously in the off-width crack – got his leg stuck. No amount of writhing could loosen it and he soon ran out of ideas and energy. Eventually, after three agonizing hours, he hacked his trouser leg off with a knife-blade piton, which allowed him to extricate himself and then down-climb. Unnerved and out of supplies, the team retreated.

Joe Brown, Martin Boysen, Mo Anthoine and Malcolm Howells returned in 1976. Boysen evened his earlier score and shortly afterwards the group stood on the summit of the incredible rocket-shaped monolith. Their route went at VI+/A2 – really hard grades for 1976, with over 20 pitches at Grade VI.

Fourteen years later this route received its first repeat – a panic-stricken one. The Japanese team of Masanori Hoshini and Satosho Kimoto had to rush up the climb in an amazing four-day, alpine-style ascent to rescue their compatriot Takeyasu Minamiura. He had soloed a new VII/5.10/A4 route on the East Face, which took 40 days, and then paraglided off the summit – only to have his canopy snag the wall 80m (260ft) from the top, leaving him hanging helplessly in space for the eight days it took his rescuers to abseil off their variant on the Norwegian route of Great Trango and reach him.

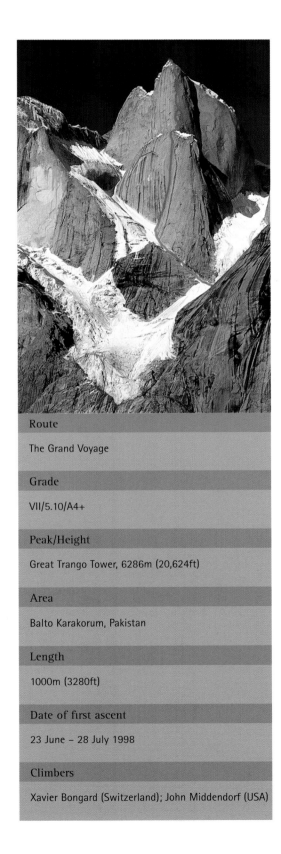

Route	
The Grand Voyage	
Grade	
VII/5.10/A4+	
Peak/Height	
Great Trango Tower, 6286m (20,624ft)	
Area	
Balto Karakorum, Pakistan	
Length	
1000m (3280ft)	
Date of first ascent	
23 June – 28 July 1998	
Climbers	
Xavier Bongard (Switzerland); John Middendorf (USA)	

Opposite The two climbers seem hopelessly tiny on the first pitches above the huge snow ledge of Grand Voyage, which at this stage, uses the Norwegian Route to gain a small crack system further up and to the right (outside this picture).

days later, obviously with minimal supplies of food and fuel left for the estimated two days required to descend. The 40-pitch climb went at Grade VII/A4 – really extreme climbing at an altitude of over 6000m (19,700ft), that required a good deal of climbing on those insecure tools of the aid climber, bat hooks and copperheads.

Sadly the summit pair died on the descent – presumably due to an abseil point failure. Their bodies were seen at the base during a helicopter search, but by the time their companions arrived at the scene, an avalanche had scoured the area. No trace of their bodies has ever been found. In his report 'Tears for Trango' (*Mountain Magazine* 111), Dag Kolstrud finishes with the words, 'The experience, achievements and victory had become quite meaningless and could give no comfort.'

An interesting insight into high-altitude big-wall climbing is given by Michel Piola, the great Swiss Alpine all-round climber, in 'Danse Trango' (*Mountain Magazine* 119): 'Tired from nearly a month of fixing the route, drunk from altitude (5800m; 19,029ft), rarely dry or warm (three of our party were getting slight frostbite), it was only by constantly providing mutual support and encouragement that we were able to retain the motivation necessary under such conditions.' Living on big walls for long periods of time is an exhausting and dangerous business – a well-knit team is essential to success. There is little doubt that John Middendorf and Xavier Bongard formed such a team.

The Nameless Tower saw a number of subsequent ascents, all noteworthy, including the East Face ED+/A3 route by Wojtek Kurtyka (Poland) and Erhart Loretan (Swiss), which was later free-climbed by Wolfgang Güllich and Bernt Arnold. On the descent, Arnold fractured his ribs and pelvis falling into a crevasse, and had to be air-lifted out – a most undignified end to a bold climb.

Amongst the most renowned of routes is the 35-pitch Eternal Flame established by the star rock-climbing duo of Kurt Albert and Wolfgang Güllich.

This stands as probably the most extreme and the most coveted climb in the Trangos, being a total free-climb at the unimaginable grade of IX- (5.12c).

The peak

The less aesthetic but higher Great Trango Tower was first ascended by Galen Rowell and an American party in 1977 via a series or rock steps and ice ramps on the South Face to the Central Summit at the relatively mild (in Trango terms at any rate) Grade of VI/A1. A 2000m (6500ft) route on the north side was soloed by Italian Maurizio Giordani in nine hours in 1988. The much less accessible East Summit was first attained by the Norwegian Route in 1984. During this phenomenal 1500m (5000ft) ascent, two of the party, Dag Kolstrud and Stein Aasheim, 'volunteered' (after much debate) to return to base after food started to run out, high on the headwall, 25 days into the climb, leaving Hans Christian Doseth and Finn Daehli to complete the route. This they did five

The route

The Grand Voyage is a 33-pitch route, 1400m (4600ft) long. It is graded VII/5.10/A4+, which makes it one of the hardest and most serious routes anywhere close to this altitude. It is located on the East Peak of Great Trango, and crosses the Norwegian Route, using four pitches of this route to link the upper and lower sections. The approach was made via the Edelweiss slope on the right bank of Trango's hanging glacier, the Dunge Glacier, then across to the base of the Norwegian Pillar.

Above Taking a risky ride over the freezing waters – one of the minor hazards of Karakorum approach marches.
Left The late Xavier Bongard, from Switzerland – one of the great Himalayan and big-wall climbers.
Opposite left John Middendorf at the first bivouac site with the fearsomely unpredictable Ali Baba's Couloir behind.
Opposite right The avalanche-prone headwall of Great Trango, capped by a heavy crown of fresh snow.

The climb was begun by following the avalanche-prone Ali Baba's Couloir (so called because it is usually closed) to a point where it cuts back to the rock. Here, Camp 2 was established under a rock canopy. The climb moved onto the wall proper, up the centre of the Norwegian Pillar to a large snow ledge and Camp 5. After this, it became necessary to use four pitches of the Norwegian route to enter another crack system, which led the pair to the right on the smooth summit wall and, via a fairly direct line, to the summit ridge. Another few rope lengths of mixed rock and deep snow led to the actual summit.

Descent was via abseil down the route, with the final descent abseils down the diamond-shaped rock slab below Ali Baba's Couloir.

The climbers

Xavier Bongard was regarded as one of the top climbers in the world. He did numerous first ascents in the mountains of his native Switzerland, and a good number further afield. He did a rapid repeat ascent of The Shield on El Capitan, as well as solo ascents of Lost in America, Sea of Dreams and Wyoming Sheep Ranch. He died tragically in 1994 on a base jump from the top of the Staubbach above Lauterbrunnen, Switzerland.

John Middendorf (USA) is best known for his big-wall climbing, particularly in Yosemite. He has pioneered over 70 big-wall and alpine-scale routes as far afield as Tasmania and the Himalayas. An engineer by trade, he was one of the chief developers of the portaledge, and still designs for North Face.

The climb

The expedition consisted of John Middendorf, photographer Ace Kvale (USA) and three Swiss nationals, Xavier Bongard, Ueli Buhler and François Studenmann. After the usual lengthy and frustrating expedition hassles in Rawalpindi and Skardu, the group finally arrived at Askole and headed off to the hills. Their gear was carried up to a base camp low on the Dunge Glacier by 46 porters. From here the four climbers started up the slopes of the Edelweiss, a spur to the right of the glacier, laying 300m (1000ft) of fixed rope for ease of ascent and descent.

'The Great Trango Tower was more awesome and fearful than we had ever imagined,' said Middendorf.

At the base of the Norwegian Pillar, the decision was made to start the route from Ali Baba's Couloir higher up. Like the thief in the story, this was full of surprises, mostly of the avalanche variety, and 'Run for your life!' became the motto of the team. At the niche in the couloir, a canopy of rock protected Camp 2, and allowed them to make a start on the rock face itself.

Bad weather set in for three days, although John and Xavier managed to set six rope lengths (a 65m/ 210ft lead rope was used). Soon after this the team split up, with Ueli, François and Ace deciding that the climbing was too technical. They returned to base camp, where Ueli and François decided to climb Nameless Tower instead, while Ace remained at base to take photographs and watch the gear.

Camp 3 was then established under an overhang at the top of pitch 5. From here on, the pair had to haul their 120kg (280 lb) of big-wall gear up with them, and were bound to their tiny portaledges.

After a good number of chimneys with tricky connecting slab moves that involved hooking and copperheading at A4, Camp 4 was set up in Gollum's Gully – named after the evil, mixed-up creature in *Lord of the Rings*: quite apt, considering the fantastic, Tolkienesque nature of the Trango area. The collapse of an overhanging cornice above resulted in minor injuries – thus for the next five pitches, until the culprit snow ledge was reached, all climbing was done once the freeze had set in after dark. The pitches involved some very delicate ice climbing, but coupled with this was the energy-sapping dragging of heavy haul sacks up the outside of the couloir. Finally, they reached the snow ledge. Middendorf describes the big-wall climbers' tensions well: 'The ability to put things down without clipping them in was a welcome relief from the previous days and nights, when everyone seemed on tenterhooks in fear of dropping items.'

The pair were now at the headwall, about halfway up the route. The section above their route had thus far proved to be totally smooth and would not accept natural gear. Refusing to stoop to placing a pure bolt ladder, they elected to use the Norwegian route until they could move onto a new line. This they soon did – after four pitches they found pitch 18, a crack that went at a desperate but fantastic A4+ with 6b sections. The cracks now widened considerably, and it became both necessary and more efficient to free-climb. The problem was that all the large camming devices had inadvertently been left with the other group, so the leading became somewhat precarious. On pitch 24, John swung off as a cam popped and the flake that came away with it landed on his finger as he hit the wall next to Xavier – narrowly missing the Swiss, who had just removed his helmet.

A succession of damp, difficult chimneys and spells of bad weather now slowed things down. Three full days later saw them only one and a half pitches higher, soaked to the skin and miserable. Then on 26 July, the sun reappeared, and they resumed climbing in earnest, up the series of metre-wide grooves on the headwall. Low temperatures made the choice of 'gloves or no gloves' and 'plastic boots or rock boots' a constant gamble. At last, pitch 33 was done, and the summit rim was attained. The pair retreated joyfully to the hanging bivouac at Camp 7, a few hundred feet below.

Opposite A fully laden John Middendorf climbing excellent snow slopes into the morning light on the lower reaches of the Great Trango Tower.
Right Adam Wainwright patiently belaying high on the Slovenian Route on Nameless Tower, from which the picture on p104 was taken.

The next day brought a much more difficult snow-and-ice ascent than they had imagined, with a lot of loose, mixed ground and chin-deep snow to wallow through. 'Just as I began to seriously doubt our chances of success, I suddenly found myself sitting on the summit, which was like the blade of a knife hidden beneath the deep snow. A final act of courage!' (Bongard, 1995)

They summitted a half-hour before sunset, and were only the second group (the other being the Norwegians, of whose gear they found traces right below the summit, confirming their ascent) to reach the summit, with most other teams turning back at the rim of the headwall.

A 1.5-hour trip down to the top of the wall, followed by a three-hour descent, brought them back to their main bivvy tent on the snow ledge.

Descent by abseil took three days, involving 44 abseils, often off single pitons. The final torture was a hair-raising set of abseils down the diamond-shaped rock slab in the centre of the gully system below the pillar to avoid the constant avalanches now streaming down Ali Baba.

In the interim, Ueli, who had broken his ankle in a fall high on Nameless Tower, and Studenmann had had an epic 36-hour nonstop descent to base camp. Bongard and Middendorf arrived just in time to bid Ueli farewell as the rescue helicopter, delayed for many days by fighting in Kashmir, arrived. The long climb was over at last.

'Finally we bathed in the security that we had so wished for up there, on the top, liberated from the prison into which we had voluntarily locked ourselves.' (Bongard)

Riders on the Storm – Paine

Where mood barometers reach the stormy zone

LYING ALMOST 170KM (105 MILES) SOUTH OF Fitzroy and the Cerro Torre group of mountains in Patagonia is the Paine group ('Paine' means 'sky-blue', and certainly applies to this area). It experiences a totally different set of weather systems, receiving less moisture than its northern counterpart. The other major difference, and one that many believe leads to the clear blue sky, is the omnipresent and fickle high winds. Gripping descriptions of the power of the wind can be found in French writer Antoine de Saint-Exupéry's book *Wind, Sand and Stars*: 'The sky was blue. Pure blue. Too pure. A hard blue sky that shone over the scraped and barren world while the fleshless vertebrae of the mountain chain flashed in the sunlight. The blue sky glittered like a newly honed knife ... Give me a good black storm in which the enemy is plainly visible.' (At this point in the writer's story, unexpected storm winds hit the mail pilot's tiny single-engined biplane and forced it to the ground.) This same clear blue sky fools climbers, too, by lulling them into a false sense of security that sees them exposed in dangerous positions.

The Paine mountain group lies on the Andes chain, which forms a barrier between two vastly contrasting worlds in the far south of the Americas. The group, lying in the carefully managed Chilean Torres del Paine National Park, is bounded by the Patagonian Ice Cap on the west, and the high, dry Pampas (rolling grasslands) in the east. When 'black storms' hit, they do so rapidly, unexpectedly and with a vengeance, throwing sleet, rain and snow at climbers. It is a region of stark beauty, the eastern side having fairytale-quality snow, ice and shale approaches, dotted with small lakelets, while the western approach gives way to Pampas with fine lakes. The American big-wall expert, Royal Robbins, after a frustrating time spent waiting for good climbing conditions, said, 'Patagonia is exceptionally beautiful: go there to hike, go there to photograph, but if you want to climb seriously you need to be a masochist with unlimited time on your hands!'

The peak

The Central Tower of Paine had an interesting nationalistic start to its climbing history. In the 1962/63 season, two teams of seasoned climbers arrived at its base – one from Italy (comprising Aste, Aiazzi, Casati, Taldo and Nusdeo), the other from the UK (composed of Bonington, Whillans, Bray, Clough, Streetly, Walker and Page). A first ascent of the 1300m (4265ft) tower was a prize much sought-after, and rivalry between the two groups was intense.

The British arrived first, and moved their tons of gear up to a base camp. They then attacked the tower from a notch left of the South Face, the Condor Col. Fierce winds hampered their efforts, and after a month they had only made 25m (80ft) of progress up the steep rock beyond the col. Their tents had been flattened, they were cold and discouraged. At this point the Italians arrived, intent on much the same route, to the annoyance of the Britons. After considerably

Route	
Riders on the Storm	
Grade	
IX/A3	
Peak/Height	
Central Tower of Paine, 2460m (8071ft)	
Area	
Southern (Chilean) Patagonia, South America	
Length	
1300m (4265ft)	
Date of first ascent	
December 1990 – January 1991	
Climbers	
Wolfgang Güllich, Norbert Batz, Kurt Albert, Bernd Arnold, Peter Dittrich (all of Germany)	

Opposite Aiding up the mildly overhanging crux system in freezing conditions on the Central Tower of Paine, this was one of the few sections where the German team had to resort to aid in place of the free-climbing they would have preferred.

tense discussions, the Italians elected to climb virtually the identical route, but agreed not to use the British ropes.

The Britons secretly began building the Whillans Box, a sort of prefabricated, livable escape from the weather, made of wood, tarpaulin and bits of metal. They moved this 113kg (248 lb) creation up to the base of the climb, while the Italians carried in their smart, reinforced tents, and both teams attempted to attack the face again. For two weeks little progress was made by either side, then the weather underwent one of its typical sudden changes, and the winds dropped to quarter-speed. Bonington and Whillans sneaked off at first light, and were soon well on their way. By the time the rest of the British team joined them, the Italians had woken up to what was going on. They swarmed out, and started to climb on the fixed ropes left by the Britons. The trailing British climbers began to pull up the ropes, increasing their lead as Bonington and Whillans frantically chugged upwards. By dint of some outstandingly bold climbing, at 17:00 they were on the summit ridge, and at 19:30 on the summit. They descended 100m (330ft), then bivouacked. The next morning they abseiled down past the sullen Italians (bar one, Taldo, who

greeted them with congratulations). The Italians were still fighting their way up, and summitted 20 hours after Bonington and Whillans.

The next major assault on the Central Tower was that of a South African group in 1974. The East Face was waiting, looming over the Torre Glacier. A prominent dihedral splits the face, a line of weakness simply asking to be climbed. Fatti, Fuggle, McGarr, Prior, Scott and Smithers proved equal to the formidable task, carving their way up the South African Route over 32 days of struggle. They referred to their climb as 'a gigantic construction project', with long and arduous aid sections. The line was sieged, with fixed ropes draping the entire face for ascent and descent, but the cold and wet conditions made using them difficult and hazardous. It was a major route, probably the longest and most serious wall climb undertaken at that time.

In 1986, Giarolli, Orlandi and Salva established Magico Est on the same East Face, and in 1992, de la Cruz (of Argentina) and Hayward and Rand (of the USA) put up El Rumbo del Viento, yet another climb to reflect the vagaries of the winds!

The climb that captured the imagination of the climbing fraternity was undoubtedly Riders on the Storm, a staggeringly difficult route on the East Face.

The climbers

Many mountaineers know Wolfgang Güllich as the world's leading sport climber, the originator of Wallstreet (XI) and Action Directe (XI). Others might know him for his on-sight solo of Separate Reality (5.11d), his second ascent of Grand Illusions (5.13c), or his role as double to Sylvester Stallone in *Cliffhanger*, just before Güllich's tragic death in a motor accident. Few know the depth and range of his climbing experiences, from an adventurous 15-year-old in 1975 to his death in 1992. In 1989 he was on the impressive almost-free ascent of Eternal Flame on the Nameless Tower (see p105–106), and in 1991, Riders of the Storm was his last major big-wall project.

Joining Güllich on the Nameless Tower climb was his long-time partner, Kurt Albert, who first gained fame as a hard sport climber, with climbs such as Exorcist (VIII) and Sauteng (X-) in the Frankenjura. He, too, is a highly respected mountaineer, with countless first and repeat ascents of various routes and peaks in Europe and abroad.

The other team members were Norbert Batz; 'hard man' East German climber Bernd Arnold, who cut his teeth on the Elbsandstein with Garten Eden (Xc), as well as on Royal Flush (Fitzroy) and Eternal Flame on the Nameless Tower; and lastly Peter Dittrich, a tall, solid climber of considerable repute.

The climb

The idea of the climb was dreamed up by Albert and Güllich after seeing images of Paine in Chris Bonington's book, *Mountaineer*. The other three German climbers needed little persuasion to join them, and they set off late in 1990.

The Patagonian weather came as a bit of a shock to the group, most of whom were hard-man free-climbers used to sunny skies and cranking desperate bolted routes. The five were fretting at having to hang around the makeshift base camp hut as vicious storms whipped the trees around them into a frenzy. The name Riders on the Storm came naturally under these circumstances.

They had originally chosen a line way on the left of the East Face, but abandoned it after watching a number of car-sized blocks hurtling down. Eventually a route further right was chosen, and the group split into two teams for convenience – Arnold and Albert; and Güllich, Batz and Dittrich.

The leaders of the two groups alternated, forging the route. The idea was to free-climb as far as possible, redpointing sections if need be. They largely managed to adhere to this philosophy, although conditions were very different to normal redpoint, short-route circumstances. Constant avalanches swept the route; the men were forced to climb in the breaking dawn; iced-up ropes made jumaring difficult and dangerous; and long hours spent belaying on tiny stances in the freezing cold frequently brought the belayer close to hypothermia.

'The pressures wearing us down make it seem as though all of our efforts and the compensation for them have slipped out of balance. Only the hope of success and luck keep us a team of dreamers and gamblers. And only dreams keep up our motivation. Dreams too have to be fed.' (Güllich)

After plugging away for weeks, they were 600m (2000ft) up the face when a band of rotten rock stopped progress. Huge chunks of granite thundered off this seam when the ice thawed, and the climbers' ropes were constantly being chopped. The teams met to decide whether to continue or retreat. Albert and Arnold agreed to have 'one last go', and on the day after Christmas, Albert took his life in his hands and jumared up the clearly damaged fixed lines. Some 30m (100ft) above one belay, he found the rope held together only by a few thin strands of mantle – just enough to hold his weight!

Two days of hair-raising climbing on friable rock with very insubstantial protection finally saw the team across the rotten band and onto solid rock. Then the weather moved in to play a more prominent role – the New Year brought freezing cold, high winds, snow and rain. As the climbers struggled up frozen cracks, they were regretfully forced to resort to aid in order to pass some of the most difficult sections.

Tensions in the team began to rise. 'The needle of our mood barometer is reaching the stormy zone,' recorded Güllich.

Many teams fragment on peaks such as Paine. Arnold wrote: 'We are on a mountain, bound to a route. The climber is a prisoner of his own goals,

and the prison walls can only be overcome by reaching the summit. Early abandonment and renunciation are not a means of escape.' The group managed to sort out its differences, and the climb continued.

The weather softened a little, and the climbing gradually became more and more free, with many pitches of up to Grade IX – an amazing grade at altitude. The giant roof which barred the way, 1000m (3000ft) off the ground, went free on only the second attempt at Grade IX. Crack lines succumbed and, finally, on 23 January, Arnold and Albert made the summit, followed four days later by the other three.

Riders on the Storm has 36 pitches, of which three are Grade IX, nine Grade VIII, and the rest mostly VII, with odd bits of aid up to Grade 3. These grades alone make it one of the hardest long routes ever climbed. The fact that it was opened in Patagonia places it in the realm of the almost mythical.

Opposite top One of the incredible flakes which allowed the German team to free-climb for hundreds of metres.
Opposite bottom Bernd Arnold puzzling out the moves on one of the difficult free sections.
Above The huge Grade IX roof-pitch, 1000m (3000ft) above the start of the climb, surrendered to the second attempt.

Slovenian Route – Cerro Torre

The toughest route in Patagonia

THE TORRES ('TORRE' MEANS PEAK) ARE located in the Fitzroy (Los Glaciares) National Park, a magnificent wilderness area located at the southern tip of Patagonia, with its western margin bordering on the great Patagonian Ice Cap. When climbers refer to the 'Torres', they are speaking of the principal three – Cerro Torre (3128m; 10,263ft), Torre Egger (2900m; 9415ft) and Torre Stanhardt (2800m; 9187ft). These lie some 3km (2 miles) southwest of the starkly beautiful Fitzroy Massif (3441m; 11,290ft), separated from it by the Torre Glacier that drains into Laguna Torre, usual site of the base camp for attempts made from the east or south. The Laguna is a sparkling blue lake, surrounded by green, flower-filled meadows. However, it is seldom seen in this state – all too often leaden grey skies, snow and howling winds characterize the area. As one frustrated Torre climber said, 'You've got to really WANT to be here to stay!'

The peak

It has been said that mountains evoke passions, and big mountains, big passions. If it were classified by the passions it has evoked, Cerro Torre should be at least around 9000m (29,500ft) high.

Few peaks have had as much drama and controversy associated with them as the Torre group, in particular the highest, Cerro Torre. Perhaps this is almost natural. The peaks themselves are tempestuous – they lie in the path of the vicious Patagonian storms that sweep in from the

ice cap, and experience some of the worst weather in the world. They are also ravishingly beautiful and, just as a beautiful woman bewitches men, so do these towers captivate the imagination of climbers. On seeing Cerro Torre during his climb of Fitzroy, Lionel Terray, one of the greatest of all French climbers, remarked, 'Now that, at least, would be worth risking one's skin for!'

The 1953 ascent by Terray and his partner, Guido Magnone, drew the attention of the climbing community to South America's Patagonian region for the first time. Cerro Torre was the obvious goal, and the Italian climbers, in particular, lusted after the plum summit. Cesarino Fava, who was living in Argentina, had seen the peak; Carlo Mauri and Walter Bonatti, too, were eyeing the coveted prize. However, Fava had the unusual handicap of having no feet. He had lost them to frostbite, through an unnecessary amputation, after his attempt on Aconcagua.

Deciding that he needed help, Fava wrote simply to 'The Spider of the Dolomites, Trento, Italy.' The letter reached its intended target: Cesare Maestri – a consummate climber, powerful, daring and technically highly skilled. Fava's letter fired him up, and he began to plan the trip. Together they explored the peak in 1958 (their arch rivals, Bonatti and Mauri, were on the West Face), but were driven off by bad weather.

Impatient Maestri quickly tired of others' inadequacies and did not, in general, get on with fellow climbers, but he liked Fava and they decided to

Route	
Slovenian Route	
— ascent --- descent	

Grade
VII/A4

Peak/Height
South Face, Cerro Torre, 3128m (10,263ft)

Area
Southern (Argentinian) Patagonia, South America

Length
1150m (3770ft)

Date of first ascent
November 1997 – January 1998

Climbers
Janez Jeglic, Silvo Karo (both of Slovenia)

Opposite On a hanging belay high up on the South Face route, the jagged dihedral which the Slovenian pair Jeglic and Karo climbed, can clearly be seen below Jeglic's stance; at this stage the granite is still broken and rather friable.

return in 1959 to attempt the North Face. Then Maestri met a young Austrian, Toni Egger, and immediately respected him for his skills on ice.

As planned, the three forged up the peak, with Fava doing amazingly well in special boots. At the Col of Conquest high on the North Ridge, however, he decided to abandon the route rather than slow the others down. Maestri and Egger climbed on, up desperate, icy slabs, until they were just below the fearsome summit mushroom. After a bivouac,

Maestri retaliated in a fashion that has sparked endless debate. In 1971, with Carlo Claus and Ezio Alimonta, he mounted an amazing siege on the peak via the southeast ridge. Using a giant compressor, he drilled 350 bolts into the rock, and reached the summit mushroom. It was so 'mushy' that he decided not climb it – so once again, the detractors denied him the first ascent!

In disgust, Maestri retired from climbing, and the world lost a stupendous mountaineer.

The route

The Slovenian Route enters the steep South Face from the huge icefield lying between El Macho and Cerro Adele. The face is mostly in shadow, and thus is even colder than cold. This has spin-offs in a reduced risk of avalanches or stonefalls, but the incessant cold can sap the energy of the climbers. The route moves from the triangular snow slope up a series of precarious icefields towards bands of rock dropping from the west pillar, and up onto the

they ploughed through it and claimed the peak. A series of abseils brought them back down to the triangular snowpatch. There tragedy struck, and Toni Egger was swept away by an avalanche.

The first Maestri controversy began, largely fueled by Mauri after he had failed on his second attempt in 1969. Had the Egger-Maestri pair really summitted by that desperate route? To date it remains unrepeated and very little evidence of their climb has ever been found (though in 1998, the Italians Giarolli and Orlandi found a possible Maestri relic at the base of the East Face dihedral high on the peak). Popular opinion robbed Maestri of what could have been (or was?) the climb of the century – a route so difficult and far ahead of what the equipment, techniques and mindset of his time allowed that it was dismissed as 'unbelievable'.

Whatever the verdict as to its legitimacy, the Compressor Route has played a major part in the ascents (and descents) of Cerro Torre. Its final few hundred metres to the summit have often been used as final pitches or the line of retreat of many other routes. The Devil's Diretissima, the Slovenian (South Face) Route, What's Love Got to do With It – all of them finish up at the Compressor Route. Numerous bad-weather descents, too, have been possible thanks to the upper bolted pitches.

southwest ridge. It then traverses a giant snowfield to meet the Compressor Route high on the southeast pillar. Descent is via this ridge.

The climbers

The Yugoslavs Janez Jeglic and Silvo Karo are two highly experienced 'Patagonian' climbers. Both had taken part in previous Yugoslav expeditions: the Great East Face of Fitzroy (Great Dihedral in 1983), the East Face of Cerro Torre (Devil's Diretissima in

Above left The southeast ridge leading up to the summit of Cerro Torre, here under typical storm conditions.
Above centre Wading through deep snow on the approach to the base of the route is an exhausting business.
Above right A tired and frozen but exultant Janez Jeglic of Slovenia on top of the wall during a storm.
Opposite Aiding up the most overhanging part of the wall: the angle at which the wall rope flies out into space gives some idea of the steepness of this, one of the crux pitches.

1985/6), the Southeast Face of Torre (Psicho Vertical in 1986) and the North Face of El Mocho (1986). Karo also played a major role in the 1987 Slovene Lhotse Shar expedition. The two had climbed together for 10 years.

The climb

Despite their experience, the Yugoslavs were intimidated by the scale of the South Face. 'It was scary, standing beneath the South Face, gazing up at the seemingly blank wall, which made the Eigerwand, Grande Jorasses and Matterhorn seem relatively easily angled.' (Karo, in *Cerro Torre Crazy*).

The pair established a snow hole near the base of the climb (tents do not long withstand the Cerro Torre winds). The first 200m (650ft) were climbed right at the beginning of November, falling ice and stones repeatedly cutting their precious ropes. (On the repeat ascents this section was always climbed before the sun rose to avoid the melting of the higher icefields.)

The weather altered constantly, which prevented the climbers from venturing back onto the route until 20 November. They had just had enough time to dig their ropes out from under the ice and complete the next (A3) section and the first of the truly dangerous pieces, an A4 on crumbling, overhanging, slabby rock, before high winds and snow forced them off again. The face was overhanging and required the advanced aid techniques of tiny copperheads, RURPs and knifeblades. Some 10 days later the weather relented, giving them a chance to return to the face where it took 14 hours of digging to find their bivouac hole. All fixed ropes had been torn away, making it desperately hard for them to climb back up, with minimum gear, to where they had stashed most of the aiding and leading equipment. Pitches that had been very hard before now presented the absolute limits of the possible. 'Only the fact that we had done this before, and knew we had, allowed us to climb this section.' After a short bit of progress, storms forced them back to base.

The 19th of December saw them back at work on the Red Band. This went through some overhangs and then a crack, too wide to take protection. A late rappel down to the bivouac and a three-hour jumar back before sunrise the next day was the team's way to make the most of this break in the weather. After managing another three hard pitches, the following night they were completely exhausted, suffering from leg cramps and headaches. The next day brought sore, frostbitten hands and feet, and the realization that they had run out of rope just before the huge roofs they knew would be the make or break of the climb.

The forced break was a relief. For days now the pair had risen well before dawn and jumared up the fixed ropes for hours, followed by mentally and physically demanding, highly technical climbing at the edge of the possible – taking nerve-wracking small falls when copperhead or hooks popped, or little flakes ripped off. Silvo Karo set off all the way back to base camp and was back by 21:00, too tired to appreciate even his birthday celebration. The next day, weather forced them back to base before any real climbing could be done.

Again the pair sat out the putrid weather, this time until 20 January, then decided to go on regardless as their visas were about to expire. They reached the giant overhang in the teeth of a hurricane-force storm, with fog so thick that visibility was down to zero. Communication between them was impossible – at one stage Janez fell 10m (33ft) and Silvo was blissfully unaware. A chunk of ice cut their rope in numerous places. They fought desperately, trying to get through the roof to the upper icefield, but whichever way they went, they found only friable rock. Eventually, while scouting about, they hit a 75-degree, steel-hard ice slope. 'Slowly, like two flies on a pane of glass, we crossed this.' When the wind ripped Silvo off the ice, Janez only just managed to stop him, right at the edge of the precipice.

In the evening they realized that they had finally reached the southeast ridge. By now their tattered rope was too short to allow the planned descent via abseil on the East Face, so they had to venture onto the unknown Maestri route, chipping the bolts out of the ice for a series of short abseils on the 50m (165ft) length of chopped and frayed rope that remained. The rappel was a tense affair, in blinding wind and snow, at well below zero, in the dark, and down an unknown route with a rope that hardly looked capable of holding up the washing, let alone a pack-laden climber. At 02:00 they finally touched ground, and found a snow hole to bivouac in.

Jim Bridwell, a true Patagonian and big-wall expert, proclaimed the Slovenian Route 'the hardest route in Patagonia' – a well-deserved accolade.

Moby Dick – Ulamertorssuaq

A masterpiece of free-climbing

GREENLAND IS A VAST ISLAND THAT CONSISTS largely of a great central ice cap rising to heights of 3000m (9850ft). Mountains surround the entire 'plate'; the Alpefjord Range lies on the south coast and the better-known Stauning Alps in the southeast. Most of the mountains on the rim have borne at least one ascent, even though climbing conditions are quite extreme, particularly in the north. Penetrating into the hills are the inlets of many fjords such as the southern Tasermuit Fjord.

Only recently has the south of Greenland seen increased mountaineering activity, most of it concentrated on the peaks east of Tasermuit. At the mouth of this long fjord lies the small fishing village of Nanortalik. Since the village has an airfield, suitable only really for helicopters but nevertheless an airfield, it is the staging post for trips to the interior. Most climbers arrive by boat from Narsarsuaq (en route careful note should be taken of the pack-ice condition, which plays a significant role in determining the limits of the climbing season).

As on Baffin (see p123), the local population is largely Inuit, but with a more Western approach to life than their Baffin cousins, and most speak Danish as their second (or, in the case of some younger Inuit, first) language.

The prime attractions in this southern region are the towers of Ulamertorssuaq and Nalumasortoq. Both consist of immaculate granite; both soar skywards with dramatic spires and huge walls.

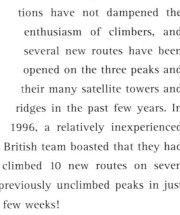

A semi-permanent glacier runs between the two, with Nalumasortoq (2045m; 6709ft) lying at the eastern limits of the glacier, a peak called Ketil to the north and Ulamertorssuaq in the south.

The region is prone to unstable weather, with storms of Arctic proportion raging suddenly and without warning across the entire island. Thus, although these towers are at a far lower altitude than equivalents such as Trango, Paine, Cerro Torre and the Alaskan peaks, they hardly fail to offer comparative experiences, because of unforeseen weather changes and low temperatures.

The fickle, icy weather conditions have not dampened the enthusiasm of climbers, and several new routes have been opened on the three peaks and their many satellite towers and ridges in the past few years. In 1996, a relatively inexperienced British team boasted that they had climbed 10 new routes on seven previously unclimbed peaks in just a few weeks!

The peak

Ulamertorssuaq has two major summits: West and East, confusingly called Right (west as seen from the glacier) and Left. At around 1830m (6000ft), West is marginally higher. It first attracted attention in 1994, leading to the establishment of Moby Dick, although a French party first climbed its big brother, Nalumasortoq, as early as 1960. Nalumasortoq is referred to as 'The El Cap of Greenland', which could make Ulamertorssuaq the 'Half Dome of Greenland'.

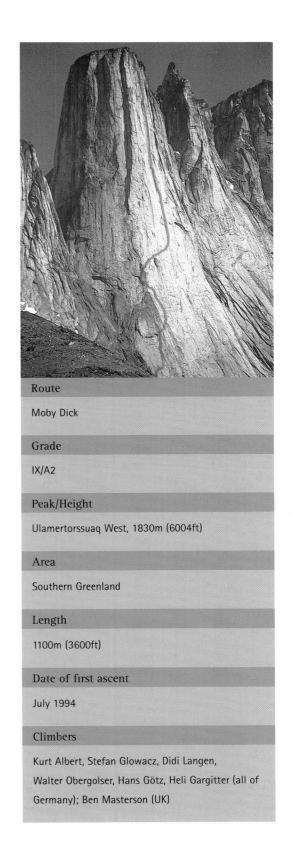

Route	
Moby Dick	
Grade	
IX/A2	
Peak/Height	
Ulamertorssuaq West, 1830m (6004ft)	
Area	
Southern Greenland	
Length	
1100m (3600ft)	
Date of first ascent	
July 1994	
Climbers	
Kurt Albert, Stefan Glowacz, Didi Langen, Walter Obergolser, Hans Götz, Heli Gargitter (all of Germany); Ben Masterson (UK)	

Opposite Superb hand-jamming follows a strenuous finger crack on the early pitches of Moby Dick, on the Ulamertorssuaq tower, Greenland. Crack systems such as this are what makes hard, free big-wall climbing both possible and pleasurable.

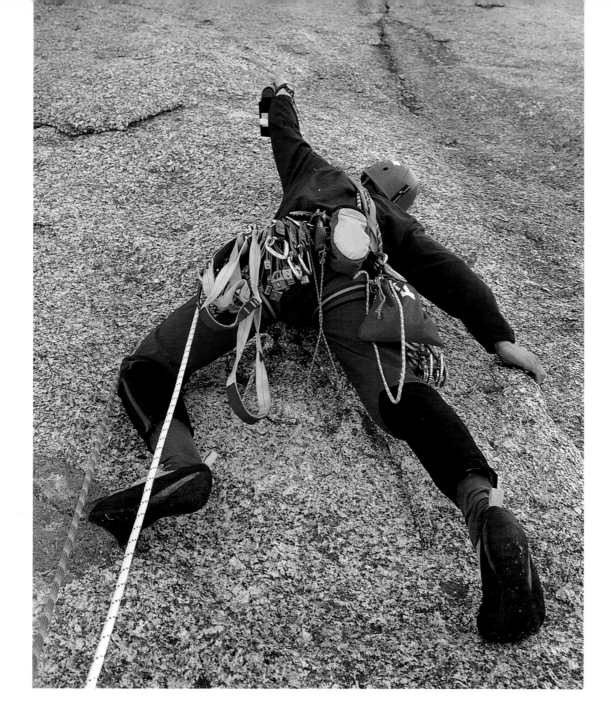

The climbers

Kurt Albert, Ben Masterson, Didi Langen, Hans Götz, Walter Obergolser, Heli Gargitter, and Stefan Glowacz made a powerful team of climbers – all German, except for Scot, Ben Masterson. One of the three most powerful members of the team was undoubtedly Glowacz, who is well known as both a sport climber (Lord of the Rings, Grade 31; Punks in the Gym, Grade 32) and a traditional climber (Strawberries, Tremadoc, E6–7/6b), and has been climbing at a high standard for almost 15 years. The other two were Kurt Albert (see p113), who has a number of impressive sport, traditional, alpine and big-wall ascents to his name, and Ben Masterson, who cut his teeth on some of the hard, traditionally protected routes in Wales and the English Lake district.

The climb

In the eyes of many of the climbing community, the ascent of Moby Dick was both a masterpiece of free-climbing and a highly controversial exercise. The group arrived in late June of 1994 and efficiently organized themselves into three teams. They began climbing on 3 July, and proceeded to climb more or less turn-and-turn-around (alternating leads) for the following 17 days. Each phase of their climb had fixed ropes, which were attached, at the end of each pitch, to good, solid bolt anchors – plenty of them. Later, when the group's very liberal use of bolts was discovered, it caused a furore.

Of interest was the redpoint ethic: each team took a turn to lead, examining, cleaning, protecting (with bolts if need be) the pitches for the day, then redpointing them. Subsequent teams then also had to get a clean redpoint to be considered to have climbed the pitches. Considering the difficulty of the route, this was an admirable decision as it demanded a great deal from each climber. One must remember that the group was comprised essentially, if not solely, of sport climbers who were used to climbing in redpoint fashion on preplaced bolts, and they saw the route as an extended free-climbing sport route. That is not to say that all of the pitches were fully bolted – the crack systems allowed for a good deal

In 1995 a British team tried the West Tower, but retreated. Next, Paul Piola put up two routes on the west flank of the tower, with a good but subtle deal of aid needed on both. In 1996, Lionel Daudet and Benoit Robert spent 13 days on the West Tower, putting up an impressive 26-pitch climb called L'Inespérée, which went largely free at F7b, with a desperate crux pitch of A4+.

Soon afterwards, Christoph Hainz and Claus Obrist added a new route, Südtiroler Profil, at Grade VIII with a IX+ crux, a 27-pitch spectacular between the two existing Piola routes, to the right of Moby Dick. The route was bolted and practised over two weeks, after which they did the free Grade IX+ ascent, making it the hardest climb in the area.

The route

Moby Dick takes a direct line up the 1100m (3600ft) west face of Ulamertorssuaq's West Tower. The climb moves up a series of off-vertical slabs at about 75 degrees, which slowly turn near vertical just over halfway up. The cracks and fissures are slightly discontinuous, but connect sufficiently to run (almost) all the way up the face. The actual climb is some 1000m (3280ft), with the rest being nerve-wracking scrambling on the lower slabs.

Above When the going gets tough, the drill has to get going. Drill-in bolts are the only feasible way to move past blank passages such as this one, much to the chagrin of the free-climbing ethos.
Opposite Free-climbing on an extremely steep section with an alarmingly blank section looming ahead.

of natural-gear placements and these, too, were frequently used. Inspections made during subsequent ascents, however, concluded that many of the bolts could be considered to have been placed superfluously. This discovery led to a great deal of controversy about large-scale bolting of adventure routes such as Moby Dick.

The climbing pattern frequently was that, while one group was climbing the new pitches, the second was repeating them after a late start from the bivouac and the third team was abseiling down to base for resupply and rest. Eventually, a halfway bivouac on a large flat ledge, mysteriously called Schwarzer Mann (black man) was established as advance base camp when the ascents up the fixed ropes proved too time-consuming and too energy-sapping. This ledge is some 400m (1300ft) above the base and from this time on the group lived on the wall through good weather and foul.

The pitches above the camp proved to be the delight of the climb – a never-ending series of cracks, ranging from tiny finger cracks to hand and fist jams, or huge body-swallowing off-width monsters that called for every crack-climbing technique in the book. The Greenland granite played havoc with the skin of the climbers, peeling it off if they were unwary or neglected to tape their hands adequately. In the icy cold, it was often difficult to feel the injuries. Only at night would the pain and the realization set in. The torture, perhaps, was more often the belayer's, who would have to sit in the cold morning or late evening, patiently and carefully feeding out or taking in rope while a partner went through the contortions and repeats necessary to claim the redpoint or laboriously drilled a hole for a bolt and hanger. Rain and wind, too, took their toll, almost causing the group to abandon its attempt on a number of occasions.

The 17th pitch proved to be the free-climbing crux, mildly overhanging with a thin jam crack running through it. After a number of rehearsals and falls had occupied the best part of a day, it eventually went free to Kurt Albert at IX+, that grade reflecting its danger and difficulty. Climbing stayed at a hard grade, with not a single pitch going below Grade VII – mostly VIII or above. By now, after two weeks on the wall, the group was weary and climbing became a cross between purgatory and automatic upward motion. Yet, they were determined to finish the route despite cold, rain and sleet. Much higher up came pitch 29, which finally broke the spirit of the team. The wonderful crack systems suddenly all blanked out, and the climbers were faced with a large, featureless, overhanging set of slabs and roofs. Numerous attempts were repulsed, and the horrible realization dawned that after all of the tortuously hard work the climb would not go free after all. No amount of throwing their exhausted bodies at the rock seemed to help. Eventually, there was no choice but to resort to placing and pulling on bolts, until the 20m (65ft) of featureless slab was beneath them. The last two pitches, thankfully, went freely and easily, and they finally stood on the summit. Exultation with a bitter taste of disappointment. A few brief hours later, the group was reunited on the Schwarzer Mann ledge, and the next day saw them revelling in the pleasures of base camp.

The route still awaits a free, on-sight attempt – yet another rock climbing problem to be solved in the new millennium!

Midgard Serpent – Mt Thor

One of the world's longest overhanging cliffs

BAFFIN ISLAND OFFERS ONE OF THE GRANDEST and most interesting climbing areas in the world. The island itself is huge (twice the size of the UK) and still largely untouched by civilization. This is the realm of the Inuit, a peaceful and resourceful people with a fascinating culture, many of whom still follow the traditional way of their forefathers, hunting seals, bears, walrus and whales. The island is incised by a series of fjords and inlets that are home to some of the largest vertical rock walls on the planet, described by Briton Eugene Fisher as '50 El Capitans, 500 Half Domes and more hard climbing than can be imagined'. (*High*, January 1995)

The fact that these expanses of rock have seen very few first ascents, and even fewer seconds in this rock-hungry world, is testimony to the island's difficult access, and its extreme climbing conditions. Winter months are cold enough to freeze the ocean solid to a depth of 2m (7ft). The short summers, from June to September, provide 24-hour daylight. The seas unfreeze and temperatures rise just enough to make climbing possible. Even then, however, there are hazards such as hungry and extremely large polar bears, a definite lack of rescue facilities and the chance that the sea will either freeze if you are there by boat, or unfreeze if you are there by sled, leaving you stranded miles from civilization.

Mt Thor is located in the Auyuittuq National Park, close to the much better known Mt Asgard. The latter gained fame from an exceptional stunt –

the ski-parachute descent by Rick Sylvester featured in the James Bond film *On Her Majesty's Secret Service*. It was also the site of the first true big-wall climb on Baffin, when Doug Scott, Paul Braithwaite, Paul Nunn and Dennis Hennek completed the 45-pitch southwest buttress in 1972 (Grade VI/5.9/A1), in an amazing 45 hours, nonstop. It was on Mt Asgard that Charlie Porter (USA) staged his incredible solo ascent of the northwest face in 1975, possibly one of the boldest ventures in the history of climbing. Having completed the 40-pitch Grade VI climb in a raging storm, with incipient frostbite, he ended up crawling for 10 days down a 60km (37-mile) fjord until he met some helpful Inuit.

The peak

Getting to Mt Thor involves a boat trip up Weasel Valley, and thereafter a 32km (20-mile) hike through tundra and over scree slopes to the base of the wall. Mt Thor is one of the largest overhanging cliffs in the world. The West Face is 1200m (3900ft) high, with the base set back well over 30m (100ft) from the summit. This natural feature made it the obvious site for the world's longest Rap/Base Jump, done (illegally, as all base jumps must be) in 1988. From the side, the peak looks somewhat like the bow of the *Titanic* just as it began to sink into the ocean (according to the film version, anyway) – a huge flat ramp leading up at a 30-degree angle to a sharp prow that falls away off-vertically back- and downwards for 1200m (3900ft).

Route	
Midgard Serpent	
Grade	
VI/5.9/A5	
Peak/Height	
West Face, Mt Thor, 1800m (5906ft)	
Area	
Baffin Island, Canadian Arctic	
Length	
1100m (3600ft)	
Date of first ascent	
July – August 1998	
Climber	
Jason 'Singer' Smith (USA) – solo second ascent	

Opposite A slightly perturbed Jason Smith contemplating the next sequence of moves from his bat tent high up on Mt Thor, Baffin Island. This picture and all those following were self-portraits, taken using remote-control methods.

third of the wall to a diagonal break. After this it wanders a little more off the direct line, with a zigzag section of traverses needed to attain the second ledge system. The real 'meat' of the route, the headwall, has an impressively straight line through a wildly overhanging set of cracks, roofs and ledges. Once the climbers reach the second section, the angle of the wall makes retreat extremely difficult, and retreat off the headwall is an absolute impossibility. The serious and committing nature of the wall made the opening pair extremely nervous at being a party of only two. One can imagine, then, the feelings experienced by the first soloist and only second ascensionist of this route, Jason Smith.

The climb

In the summer of 1997, Americans Chris McNamara and Jason Smith travelled to the Weasel Valley to climb Mt Turnweather. That peak seemed to have an 'overabundance' of waterfalls and rock coming down its face, so the pair headed off for Mt Thor to attempt the Midgard Serpent. They managed only two pitches before time and lack of rations forced them to turn back. In mid-July of 1998 Smith was back with a solo ascent in mind. In April he had shipped half of his supplies to Windy Lake; when he arrived in July, it took two days of to-ing and fro-ing to carry the rest of his supplies there, followed by seven days of walking the 16km (10-mile) distance to and from the wall with heavy packs. Smith likened progress on the tundra to walking on a soft, thick, wet feather bed. The steep scree field to the base of the wall, strewn with loose boulders, added to his torture. Eventually, the tortuous walking was over, and the climb itself could begin.

After 10 days of glorious weather, as he started up the cliff, it started to snow, with ice eventually falling from above. Ignoring this as best he could, Jason moved rapidly up the first few pitches, then began hauling the 180kg (400 lb) of haul bags containing all his gear up to the bivouac site. It took three hours of extreme effort, despite a pulley system. He solo-ed two more overhanging pitches, and abseiled down to his overnight site, exhausted.

Two days of hard climbing later, while hauling his kit up the wall for an epic eight hours, a huge block of ice trundled off just next to him. Jason recalls that it took him 10 minutes of staring into space before he could respond by jettisoning

In 1985 a group of Americans under the driving force of Earl Redfern made an epic 35-day capsule-style (see p129) ascent of the face, giving it the first Grade VII rating for any North American climb (VII/5.10/A4). The party consisted of Eric Brand, Tom Bepler and John Bagley.

Of considerable interest is a 30-pitch climb on the left buttress, which avoids the main overhangs, done entirely by the local Inuit, using a good deal of borrowed gear and plenty of initiative. Later, a Spanish team put up a Grade VI with 'some aid' on the right side of the face – it was quite a bit of aid, considering the 260 holes that they left behind!

The route

In 1995 John Rzeczycki and Brad Jarrett, two 'big-wall freaks', headed for the huge Thor West Face. The idea was to put a diretissima up the centre of the face, using as much natural protection and few bolts as possible. This they succeeded in doing during 15 24-hour days in August. The Grade VI/A4 route was climbed in 20 long pitches, capsule-style. In order to beat the weather (which, fortunately, held off until just after the climb), they spent long days on the wall. The climb can, for convenience, be broken into three sections. The first follows a series of tenuous cracks in a more-or-less straight line up the bottom

20 litres (4gal) of water – a delayed response that made him realize how exhausted he was. The saving in weight increased his commitment: the route now had to be finished in a time window dictated by his supplies of water and food.

The following day, Jason took a 15m (50ft) fall when a small flake pulled during an aiding section and he burned his fingers on the rope. He had to tape them together to allow him to use his hand. The next day, he felt completely unmotivated until a book on psychology (part of his heavy haul bag) inspired him: '...the act you are presently engaged in might be your very last act ... when you hesitate, you are acting as though you might be immortal'. Within minutes he was back on the wall, relying on marginal protection, standing on precarious hooks, soon to take another fall – this time with a smile.

Traverses that constitute a menace for standard parties are a treble sword for the soloist, because he has to negotiate them three times. The 13th pitch was a 30m (100ft) 5.9 traverse over rotten granite, and bringing the haul bags across needed a virtual fourth repeat of the section. Smith looks on this as one of the most difficult parts of his ascent. Looking at the ledge below, he noticed abandoned haul bags – the legacy of Go Abe, the Japanese who had died during his solo attempt the previous year. To cap the feeling of gloom and doom, it began to snow heavily. That night, Jason started to have hallucinations – hearing first a nonexistent rockfall, then the alarm of his long-since defunct watch.

The next day he climbed a long and serious expanding flake, and his diary that night records: 'I feel like my head is nuked.' The hallucinations persisted. As he put it, 'both my psyche and the weather deteriorated rapidly.' The bugbear of the long-haul solo climber had struck – the mental fight was on as lack of human companionship began to bite. Jason was now on the headwall, which was both steep and sustained. He found that Grigris and iced ropes did not go together, and had to rethink his method of solo-protecting.

The discipline demanded by big-wall climbing was starting to be irksome, and his strict routine was decaying rapidly; on a big wall nothing can be left lying around, everything must be clipped in, neatly ordered and accessible – dropping the stove could spell a life-threatening situation. Climbing during the day was tense, on precarious points of aid, with a fall constantly in mind. The free-climbing was always risky and difficult, mentally and physically, in the knowledge that there was no belayer to aid escape from a fall. On the high, hanging bivouac, constant vigilance was necessary.

Eventually, almost as if by accident, he climbed a free pitch, found no more rock towering above him and stumbled onto the summit ridge, legs unwilling to walk after 13 days on the wall. 'Even though I was miles from shelter, just being untied from the ropes felt like a new life.'

Getting down from Thor is not easy. Jason jettisoned his haul bags by parachute, then staggered through a driving blizzard down a scree slope, looking for ropes he hoped were still in place from the original ascent. Eventually the 200m (656ft) of rope was found, and he descended. Halfway down, to his horror, the exposed core of the rope glared at him. Somehow he managed to pass the frayed section, then abseiled nervously down the iced-up rope to a gully at the top of a 25m (80ft) cliff. There were no ropes in place, the gully was streaming with icy water and getting down involved hair-raising soloing. A number of times he had no choice but to slide straight down until he could grab a chockstone, the void always looming below. At 13:00 he reached level ground, and promptly piled into his bivvy bag for a 12-hour sleep.

Jason Smith had successfully completed a true solo ascent of one of the most difficult big-wall climbs in the world, in one of the most extreme areas – quite an achievement for a young climber, in his own words, 'sort of touching twenty'.

Opposite top Jason Smith carrying the final of many tiring loads up the scree slope to the base of the wall.
Opposite bottom A room with a view – a well-organized hanging bivvy in good weather conditions.
Top The solo climber cooking up a storm on the portaledge, now sporting its bad-weather canopy.
Right 'I took this photo in case all went wrong; people might have a good idea what had happened'. A self-portrait taken just before setting out on the dangerous rappel descent.

Big Mountain Climbs

Hateja. Golden Pillar. Gaurishankar West Face. Changabang North Face. Lhotse South Face. K2 South Face.

'The most beautiful line I have ever seen'

Mick Fowler talking about Spantik

THE TERM 'BIG MOUNTAIN' IS generally understood to include any imposing peak with a height of at least 5000m (16,400ft). All of the mountains in this group are considered to be 'high altitude' and they all present climbers with unique challenges that are not experienced on similar climbs done at lower heights. Altitude affects not only a climber's performance but also his or her ability to reason logically. Any extended period of time spent above a 'personal baseline' that may vary from below 5000m (16,400ft) to well above 6000m (19,700ft) can have seriously debilitating effects.

Although all of the peaks in this chapter, apart from Lhotse and K2, fall below the 'magic' 8000m (26,250ft) line, there can be no doubt about their Big Mountain status. Beatrice, for example, is only 5800m (19,030ft) high, but experiences the type of winds normally associated with high altitudes, as well as Himalayan storms. Similarly, the glacier approaches, longish walk-in and dangerous séracs, all serve as ample qualification.

Expeditionary, alpine and capsule climbing styles

The expeditionary approach to big mountains gives climbers time to acclimatize to altitude. This is achieved via constant trips up and down, to establish a route and stock advanced camps with supplies. The success of the climb depends on a large team which establishes subcamps along the route. Not all of the members of this team are expected to reach the summit, which can lead to clashes and rivalry. The expeditionary approach is becoming more and more rare nowadays, because sponsorship is increasingly difficult to find. The very inaccessibility of some peaks, as well as the difficulty of the route, however, may still demand it occasionally. Often lightweight attempts ride on the back of larger expeditions, relying on their trail breaking or obtaining their support to carry supplies up to advance camps.

In the other two increasingly popular and closely related styles a small group of committed, equally experienced climbers moves along their chosen route as fast as possible to avoid altitude problems. The clear advantage of speed can be seen in feats such as Benoit Chamoux's successful 23-hour ascent of the Abruzzi Spur of K2 in 1986, which was done in the same season in which 13 slower-moving climbers perished.

In an alpine-style approach, the climbers shun up-and-down forays. Instead they carry all of the equipment that is required and climb in one continuous 'push'. It is usual for all of the members to attempt to summit, and oxygen is not used. Camps may be established on the way up and are usually left in place to be used as retreats on the way down, rather than being constantly visited for repeat forays.

Capsule-style climbing refers to some of the more challenging routes that may involve preliminary load-carrying to higher camps, although travel is still light and fast, using no porters.

The most difficult routes are completed in these styles, which embody all the elements of extreme climbing – commitment, risk, physical effort, adventure, and personal satisfaction.

Previous pages Climbers approaching the summit of K2, Karakorum, via the North Ridge during a 1996 expedition.
Opposite, left to right High altitude and deep snow make progress in the Karakorum difficult and slow; ascending fixed ropes during the 1996 ascent of the north ridge of K2; the ridge looks deceptively easy, but at this altitude even the smallest movement becomes a major task and nothing is ever easy.
Right Walking back to base camp with the steep face of Beatrice, Pakistan, just visible on the left.

Hateja – Beatrice

Boys to the right, girls to the left

BEATRICE IS LOCATED IN THE PAKISTANI PART of the Karakorum Range (see p135), above the scenic Charakusa Glacier, which drains the southern slopes of K6 (6934m; 22,753ft) and K7 (7000m; 22,967ft) among other peaks. The mountain, named after Princess Beatrice, the young daughter of the British Royal Family's Prince Andrew ('because it is short and dumpy') is actually an imposing and attractive peak, despite the description given by David Pickles and Bob Marks, the pair who made the first ascent. They admit to also having named it in honour of British climber Beatrice Tomasson (see p71). The peak is in a little-known area of the Karakorum, with the nearest major peak, Chogolisa, a good few kilometres distant.

The Southeast Face of Beatrice has a huge granite wall projecting through the snow, with a series of appealing crack lines running up the face. These features fired the imagination of an all-female climbing group, an added attraction being that this was a technically difficult route – and it was on the first Himalayan Peak to be named after a woman.

The route

The Southeast Face rears up from Charakusa Glacier for 800m (2600ft) in an unbroken sweep of immaculate golden granite. With a starting height of over 5000m (16,400ft), and a summit height of just under 6000m (19,700ft), it is somewhat more than Alpine in scale. The face itself is in the league of big walls such as those of Yosemite, but with additional hazards imposed by glaciers; snow and ice on the approaches, faces and summit; and an altitude that can cause problems.

The route proper starts at a ledge 150m (500ft) up the wall (where the first pitches were shared with an accompanying group of male climbers). A left-leaning ramp is followed to a corner, with free-climbing of 6a. After some 200m (650ft), a set of loose blocks leads to an overhanging ice-filled dihedral and couloir that require considerable aid. A series of diagonal moves to the left, going from crack system to crack system, leads to fault lines that exit onto the summit via snow- and icefields and a final set of loose, overhanging blocks near the very top of the climb.

The climbers

Louise Thomas has made a name for herself on a number of long and difficult routes, including the American Direct on the Dru (in a day) and The Nose of El Capitan, as well as the Shield Route and the Salathé Wall, two major routes in Patagonia. She also accomplished the second ascent of Moby Dick (see pp119–121) and the first ascent of Umwelten, a difficult 700m (2300ft) route on Nalumasortoq. To this can be added a high degree of proficiency on ice gathered in her native Scotland, as well as Wales, Canada and France, and rock climbing at a grade of E5. Louise is one of only a few female UIAGM mountain guides. She is a climbing instructor at the British National Centre, Plas-Y-Brenin, in Wales.

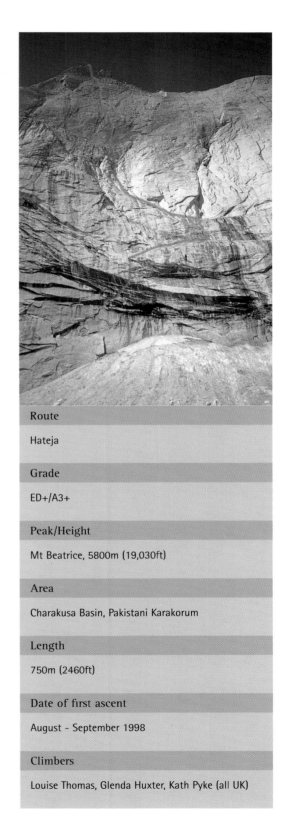

Route
Hateja

Grade
ED+/A3+

Peak/Height
Mt Beatrice, 5800m (19,030ft)

Area
Charakusa Basin, Pakistani Karakorum

Length
750m (2460ft)

Date of first ascent
August - September 1998

Climbers
Louise Thomas, Glenda Huxter, Kath Pyke (all UK)

Opposite On the day of the final summit-bid on Beatrice, Kath Pyke looks down onto Louise Thomas and Glenda Huxter, who is jumaring up the fixed lines from the bivouac below. Much further below, portaledges can be seen.

three expert climbers were eminently suited to attempt a hard, technical, new big-wall and big-mountain route on a high peak.

The three women were accompanied by three highly experienced male climbers from the UK, Mike (Twid) Turner, Grant Farquhar and Steve Mayers, with whom each had previously climbed on various occasions. The intention was to share only logistics and travel, but do two totally separate routes on Beatrice.

The climb

To some extent, the climb really started on the approach march as the three women had never climbed together and still had to get to know each other. Being female climbers, visiting a Muslim country imposed certain restrictive confines, but they were very careful to observe dress and behavioural customs in the towns and cities, and their initial doubts proved to be unfounded.

After some substantial load-carrying, the two teams arrived at 4100m (13,450ft) – base camp in an area of gentle meadows and gurgling streams. The next day saw them moving up, over loose and difficult scree slopes, to the site of advance base camp, still quite a few hours from the base of the huge wall. At this stage, Glenda, Kath, Twid and Grant experienced heat and altitude problems and were forced to retreat back to base camp.

Louise and Steve moved up to the wall to look for the two routes. Careful examination revealed only one line of weakness in the lower reaches, a viciously overhanging crack terminating in a set of wild roofs. In Louise's words, 'There is always a good reason why something so stunning has remained untouched!'

After much debate, and an attempt to keep the two routes completely separate by using a corner (that proved to be under constant threat from ice and stone falls), it was eventually agreed that the only possible solution was for the male and female groups to work together on the lower crack line, and branch off as soon as possible thereafter.

Briton Glenda Huxter is perhaps best known for her rock-climbing exploits, which include the first female ascents of The Bells, The Bells (E7) at Gogarth in Wales, Lord of the Flies (E6/6b) on Dinas Cromlech, and the ascent of Care in the Community (E5), also at Gogarth, which presented the first female- as well as traditional-led ascent of an E5. The name of this last climb is of particular relevance as Glenda teaches outdoor activities to people with learning disabilities. Her long-route experience includes the Salathé Wall and The Nose in Yosemite, Washington Column's southeast Face, and the Half Dome. She is a phenomenal rock climber, bold and committed.

Fellow Briton Kath Pyke, likewise, is a determined and practised climber with both rock- and alpine-climbing experiences behind her. These

Top Approaching the base of the route over the glacier, the tiredness of the leader is evident.

Left Louise Thomas leading up one of the magnificent crack systems with a huge rack of gear.

Opposite left Louise and Glenda organizing a meal at the bivouac spot, hundreds of feet above the glacier.

Opposite right Louise, Glenda and Kath smile triumphantly on the summit ridge, just before their long descent.

When the weather relented, all six trudged up to advance base camp (ABC), full of restored energy and enthusiasm for the task ahead. Yet, the deep new snow on the trail exhausted them, and when they reached ABC they discovered that one of their tents had collapsed, while the other was completely buried. They retreated to base for a further day of recovery. The next day saw renewed efforts to head back up to advance base. When they reached it in the late afternoon, a decision was made to jumar up to the bivvy ledge that had now become slippery with snow and ice. Equipment stored on the ledge had been buried under tons of snow, and it was late that night before they slept.

After reorganizing the camp the next morning, they set off on their respective routes – boys to the right, girls to the left. Glenda led the first rock pitches at 5b, over loose rock to a more solid corner. After this auspicious start, the rhythm of climbing on a big wall quickly established itself – two would jumar up and climb, the other would spend the day, or part of it, on the bivvy ledge, cooking, resting and organizing gear.

Their route lay mostly in the shade and was very cold, with a constant shower of rocks and ice flying down the face from sunlit ledges above. A dangerous, ice-filled couloir had to be negotiated directly in the firing line. Glenda led this minimally protected 6a section. The following day a steep, icy corner was led at A3+, their pegs constantly ripping, and the final 30m (100ft) or so was done only on tiny P-nuts and RPs. As a result, their progress was excruciatingly slow, particularly, one would imagine, to the frozen belayers standing, or hanging, for hours on tiny stances.

A retreat to the base followed, to view the top of the route and rest briefly. On the Sunday, Kath and Louise started up early only to get trapped on frozen ropes in a downpour followed by snow. The rest sensibly retreated to base. Jumars eventually failed to work on the iced-up ropes and it became necessary to prussik – a tedious process at the best of times, but 10 times worse for climbers in the advanced stages of hypothermia.

Tuesday they were back at work, inching upward on tenuous aid, then managing a glorious bit of free-climbing, before having to tackle the next frustratingly slow aid sections. The final few days of push began in earnest. 'Glenda moved left to the flakes, easy climbing drawing her away from the solace of protection in the cracks, while scary moves drove her back to find a belay.' Thursday was their last day before they would have to retreat, because of porters and expiring permits. Yet, unknown ground lay ahead.

By now, the team of women was spectacularly tired and knew that it was down to a do-or-die push. Moving as fast as they could, or dared, they shoved on, relying on tenuous anchors and sparse belays. The climb went into an ominously black fault line, which fortunately gave way to a final corner and steep cracks leading between a series of overhanging blocks to the summit. By around 18:00 that evening, the team was standing on the tiny summit pinnacle. 'We wanted to stay. We wanted this moment to last for as long as possible – but, as ever, darkness made its call.'

The top was not the end, of course. What remained was to abseil down the huge face, cleaning off as much gear as possible. Then the vast mound of collected gear had to be carried over the slippery, treacherous glacier back to base camp within a day, in order to make their timetable.

On her way down with a full load, Glenda, bringing up the rear, nearly abseiled onto a stripped rope that would never have held her. Fortunately, she was carrying rope from higher up and could replace the section. Finally, the three proud women were reunited with the male team, who had successfully completed their route, The Excellent Adventure (750m/2460ft; ED+/A3+). A fine pair of results for the Joint North Wales Expedition.

Hordes of crevasses made the glacier approach both difficult and dangerous. Each time the teams negotiated it, new ones seemed to have arrived. The overhanging crack and ledges were led in turn, first by Twid, then by Louise, with the large roof falling to her. It was turned with the aid of a 'groaning, downward-leaning knifeblade piton' and a number-one RP – the tiniest of all metal wedges – hardly something anyone would choose to carry an adult's full weight through an extensive roof move. Steve led the next section, which consisted of crumbling ledges that offered no possible belay placements for a belay on a full rope length. Then the group abseiled off.

On their return the following day, Grant and then Kath led the next pitches to a sloping bivvy ledge. That night they retreated to the advance base tents and the next day was spent carrying loads up to the base of the wall and resting. When a cold front descended, everyone was forced back to base camp. For eight days it snowed, rained and avalanched. Several feet of new snow made both the approach and the climb much more hazardous.

Golden Pillar – Spantik

A strange combination of aesthetics and lunacy

THE KARAKORUM IS A LARGE AND COMPLEX set of peaks, valleys and glaciers lying at the western end of the Himalayan range. It is usually divided into the Greater and Lesser Karakorum, with the former holding the highest Karakorum peaks: the Gasherbrums (8068m/26,471ft and 8035m/26,363ft), Broad Peak (8047m; 26,402ft) and K2 (8611m; 28,252ft), as well as Kunyang Kish (7852m; 25,762ft), Distaghil Sar (7885m; 25,870ft) and Bojohangur, or Ultar (7388m; 24,240ft).

The Lesser Karakorum has peaks such as Rakaposhi (7788m; 25,552ft) and Masherbrum, which attains a height of 7821m (25,660ft), as well as a superb set of peaks around the 7000m (23,000ft) mark.

Politically speaking, the Karakorum is part of Kashmir, but Pakistan has claim to most of the peaks. Although the Karakorum Highway has altered the nature of the area to some extent, there are still many wild and unexplored places remaining for the adventurous traveller, and several peaks below 7000m (22,970ft) await first ascents, particularly in the more remote wilderness.

Immense and beautiful glaciers, such as Baltoro (which is flanked by 10 of the world's 30 highest peaks), lie within the Karakorum. There are also the Batura, Hispar, Biafo and Barpu glaciers, above which looms the peak of Spantik.

The latter peak lies a short distance of 30km (18 miles) from the Karakorum Highway, but is accessible only via a rugged jeep track to Nagar, which leads precariously on to Hoppar, a tiny village on the very edge of the confluence of the Bualtar and Barpu glaciers. A subsequent strenuous 35km (22-mile) walk-in has, thus far, deterred idle trippers.

The mountain

At 7028m (23,059ft), Spantik cannot be classed one of the Himalayan giants. Sitting, as it does, in the middle of the range, the peak is not easily spotted, and it was only in 1906 that famous Fanny Bullock Workman, with 58-year-old husband William in tow, made an attempt on the peak's long Southeast Ridge from the head of the Chogo Lungma Glacier. They climbed up to 6700m (22,000ft), but had to turn back due to bad weather. It was only 49 years later, in 1955, that a German expedition under Karl Kramer finally reached the summit via the Workman route.

Numerous other expeditions followed thereafter, all via the Chogo Lungma.

The route

The most obvious reason to climb a mountain is to be the first to reach the top. Climbers may also choose to repeat a route as a challenge, or to improve on the climbing style of the first ascensionist. A different motivation exists for climbers who want their own share of the glory and recognition that goes with being the first to do an entirely new route up an already climbed peak.

Route	
Golden Pillar	
Grade	
ED+/VI (Scottish grading)	
Peak/Height	
Northwest Face, Spantik, 7028m (23,059ft)	
Area	
Hispar Karakorum	
Length	
2100m (6900ft)	
Date of first ascent	
5–11 August 1987	
Climbers	
Mick Fowler, Victor Saunders (both of the UK)	

Opposite Briton Vic Saunders doing some interesting, but hard, mixed-climbing up the eighth pitch of the Golden Pillar on the second day of his ascent. Note the sling draped, somewhat precariously, over a nubbin of rock.

There is yet another reason, a rather strange combination of aesthetics and lunacy: the desire to climb a route because it is 'the most beautiful line I have ever seen'. These words were uttered by Briton Mick Fowler to describe the Golden Pillar of Spantik. It was the exquisite and compelling nature of the route that motivated the somewhat do-or-die attempt by Fowler and Vic Saunders (UK).

The pillar is a towering mass of rock and ice that looks almost out of place on the slender summit cone of Spantik. Climbers sometimes compare the grandeur of this feature with the great lines of

Walker Spur in the European Alps, or the Frêney Pillars, the northeast pillar of the Droites in the French Alps. In terms of appearance they are possibly justified, but in terms of scale they are way out. Walker Spur, for instance, starts at 3000m (9800ft) and finishes a scant 1000m (3000ft) later, while the Golden Pillar rises at 4700m (15,500ft) and is twice as long as Walker, topping out – after a staggering 2100m (7000ft) – at a height of 6800m (22,300ft).

The route follows the obvious line of the pillar. It starts to the left, in a broad snow gully, and moves onto the serpentine arête of snow that climbs to the base of the final 1100m (3600ft) of the pillar. The climb moves over the hanging glacier to the amphitheatre, and then via a set of chimneys to the right-hand edge of the pillar. Snow-covered rock and ramps lead back towards the summit, with a final set of chimneys and ice gullies bringing them to the dramatic climactic open-book pitch at Grade VI (all grades given are Scottish) that culminates in a huge hanging sérac, the Ice Ear. Once this is surmounted, a further 200m (650ft) remain to the summit. Descent is via the Southwest Ridge to 6500m (21,300ft), from where a snowy spur leads back to the glacier.

The climbers

Mick Fowler is a prolific climber, accomplished over a number of decades doing a wide range of climbing styles – from short routes like the gritstone Linden on Curbar, and Heart of Gold on the sea cliffs of Gogarth to the ice/mixed route Shield Direct on Ben Nevis and the sea cliffs of Ireland and Corsica. Sea cliffs, from Dover in his native England to 'similar crumbling horrors' elsewhere (to quote Pat Littlejohn, a one-time partner), seem to be one of the loves of Mick's life. His climbing experience in the greater ranges includes Ushba in the Caucasus (1986), Hunza in the Karakorum, and the South Face of Taulliraju in Peru. Spantik, in 1987, was followed by the North Face of Ak Su in Russia, among other achievements.

Lured by a love for mountains, Victor Saunders gave up his career as an architect to become a full-time mountaineer. His extensive experience had its beginnings in the Alps and also includes epic climbs on the West Face of Makulu II, the hidden pillar on Bojohangur (Ultar), and the dramatic Panch Chuli V climb, during which Stephen Venables broke his legs and Chris Bonington fell while assisting him. Vic's penchant is for alpine-style ascents on big mountains in the 'best possible style'. Last but not least, he is also known for his incisive dry wit and tongue-in-cheek writing about his (and others') exploits in books such as *No Place to Fall* and *Elusive Summits*.

The climb

Alpine-style climbing takes on new dimensions on a pillar the size of Spantik. It is one thing to pack enough food and fuel for a few days on the slopes of Mont Blanc, but quite another to envisage the number of days it might take to complete 2100m (6890ft) of desperately hard climbing at altitude. However, alpine-style it was going to be, with one or two small differences. The first concerned a short exploration of the proposed descent route, down a spur some 1500m (5000ft) west of the Golden Pillar. The second involved a series of retreats to base camp, necessitated by bad weather.

From advance base camp just under the pillar, the initial gullies (Grade II/III) went rapidly to the experienced pair, as did the long snow arête. Thereafter, a tricky, mixed step led onto the central hanging glacier, which they disposed of rapidly. The end of the first day consisted of fixing two pitches on the actual pillar itself, before retreating to base camp in the face of deteriorating weather.

It was a few days before Fowler and Saunders could resume the climb, and the duo moved swiftly up over the fresh powder snow to their previous high point where they had stored their gear. A further delicate eight pitches (Grade IV/V) on the snow-plastered rock on the front of Spantik's pillar brought them to the Amphitheatre, an icefield similar in aspect to the notorious Spider on the North Face of the Eiger. Excavating behind a flake, they created a tiny, but viable bivouac ledge.

From their airy perch, a chimney line led off to the right edge of the pillar. First, however, came a pitch at Grade VI. At this point, the thin, indeter-

Above The route runs up the snow slope directly right of the cairn, onto the sinuous ridge, then onto the pillar itself.
Opposite top Mick Fowler approaches the ominous sérac that bars the way to the top of the Golden Pillar.
Opposite centre (left to right) Vic Saunders, Rajab the cook, and Mick Fowler after completing the climb.
Opposite bottom A cheerful Saunders stands at the top of the descent ridge from the summit of Spantik. The much sought-after peak of then unclimbed Bojohangur (Ultar) dominates the skyline in the centre background.

minate smears of ice on the surface of the pillar's upper reaches revealed, not the granite that the pair of climbers had assumed the Golden Pillar was composed of (as with most of the Karakorum) but instead, a very compact form of pinkish marble that offered disconcertingly few cracks for protection and was extremely smooth and slippery under snow. Next came Mick's forte – some loose shale in a gully, which led to the next bivouac ledge.

The next day saw them moving across 60-degree slabs under a thick coating of powder snow; nerve-wracking work, with the surface often invisible and the precious few cracks hard to find. Protection on this section was, to say the least, sparse. At last a vertical corner led up to a giant jammed block, site of the next bivouac. The following day consisted largely of aid-climbing up overhanging grooves to another series of slabs and ramps. Here, an unprotected chimney (Grade V) led up to an ice shield. At the top of this pitch, Saunders could find nowhere to place gear, so he wedged himself across the gap and, with the caution 'Don't fall off!', brought his partner up. It was while climbing this section that they realized there was no way in which their route could be reversed – it was the top, or nothing.

The day ended in a hanging bivouac at the centre of a huge ice ramp, suspended off a single nut placed in the only crack they had been able to find. The next day saw little improvement in protection,

and increasingly hard climbing. The climb on the pillar finished in grand style – an open-book corner at Grade VI, positioned under the vast hanging sérac, the Ice Ear. After scuttling left past it, they ploughed through deep snow to a well-deserved horizontal bivouac. Most of the following day was again spent churning through waist-deep snow, over easy but frustrating ground. A final vertical 200m (650ft) to the summit, and they reached their bivouac at the top by dark.

Of interest here, is the resolute determination of the pair to fully complete the entire route to the summit. Some modern climbers consider a climb to be complete once the difficult sections have been done. This has led to controversy in the climbing fraternity, and has already resulted in ascents being denied to parties who stopped short of the summit (see also p99–100).

If the way up had been difficult, the descent was no picnic either. The route down, via the Southwest Ridge and the spur, led over many cornices and large sections of avalanche-prone windslab. This potential hazard meant that the exhausted climbers could not relax for a moment until they had regained advance base camp. Only after eight days of nonstop extreme effort were they finally able to collapse in the safety of the base camp tent.

This is recognized as one of the most difficult climbs ever in the Karakorum, with over 20 pitches of Scottish Grade V and above. Many sections could not be down-climbed and abseiling was impossible given the lack of protection; it was a case of total commitment. A subsequent party, attempting the Golden Pillar by placing bolts on its lower sections, was mercifully driven off by bad weather. This type of ascent was certainly not in keeping with the pure ethic of the opening ascensionists, and one hopes that future climbers will respect serious routes and climb them in the intended style – that is, without the artificial security of bolts. These routes are only for those who are willing to risk the vagaries of bad weather and poor protection.

West Face – Gaurishankar

A summit that's twice-holy

THE MOUNTAIN GAURISHANKAR LIES ON THE border of Nepal and Tibet. With its twin summits towering over the valley, it is a most impressive landmark when seen from the ancient Nepalese capital, Kathmandu. Until expeditions were mounted to the inner Himalayas and surveyors proved otherwise, many regarded it as the highest in the world. Buddhist monks, who see only the south summit from their monastery at Sola Khumbu, call it *Jomo Tseringma* ('the holy one'). Nepalese Hindus call the higher north summit *Shankar*, a variant form of Shiva, god of creation and destruction. The lower summit is named *Gauri*, for the golden goddess, Shiva's consort. Thus, the mountain has double holy status, and for this reason has frequently been off-limits to climbing expeditions.

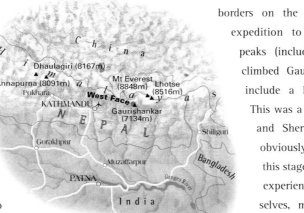

Politics and border warfare have also limited access to the peaks of the Nepal Himalayas, which include Mt Everest, Annapurna, Kangchenjunga and Dhaulagiri. Nepal's policy of excluding foreign climbers lasted until 1949, while the Tibetan policy was in force even longer. In the early 1950s, Raymond Lambert approached (illegally) from the Tibetan side, and pronounced Gaurishankar unclimbable. Still today no-one has proved him wrong – the steep and forbidding East Face he observed has yet to be conquered.

In 1959, a large Japanese expedition foundered in their attempt on the peak. Five years later, a British team under Dennis Gray made an epic trek up the densely forested Rongshar Gorge to the foot of the northwest ridge. They got up to 7000m (23,000ft), and were even forced to make an illegal traverse onto the Tibetan side of the ridge before a series of avalanches forced them off. The arrival of the monsoon put a final cap on their effort. This attempt was followed by the general closure of mountaineering on Nepalese peaks, which, coupled with the political unrest in Tibet at the time, meant that Gaurishankar was effectively off-limits.

In 1979, Nepal once again opened its borders on the proviso that any expedition to certain specified peaks (including the yet unclimbed Gaurishankar) had to include a Nepalese national. This was a reasonable request and Sherpas, in particular, obviously fitted the bill. By this stage many were highly experienced climbers themselves, more than able to hold their own on expeditions. Al Read, the American director of a firm that called itself Mountain Travel Nepal, managed to obtain a permit for the first spring season, and quickly assembled an expedition to attempt the peak.

The climbers

John Roskelley has been part of the American climbing scene for many years. Many of his earlier ascents were done with the likes of Jim Bridwell, renowned for his work on the big walls of Yosemite and the Canadian-Alaskan Mountains. In 1984, Roskelley attempted an almost successful alpine-style ascent of the unforgiving

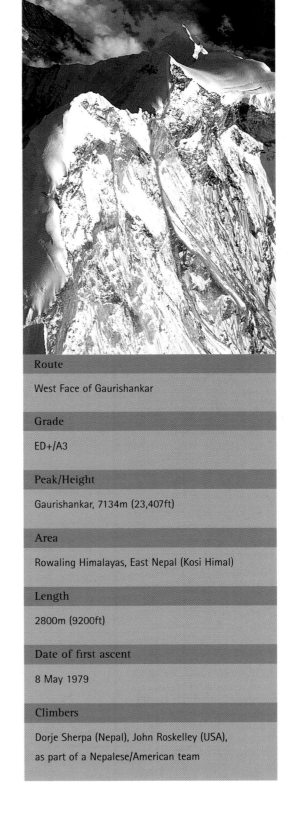

Route	
West Face of Gaurishankar	
Grade	
ED+/A3	
Peak/Height	
Gaurishankar, 7134m (23,407ft)	
Area	
Rowaling Himalayas, East Nepal (Kosi Himal)	
Length	
2800m (9200ft)	
Date of first ascent	
8 May 1979	
Climbers	
Dorje Sherpa (Nepal), John Roskelley (USA), as part of a Nepalese/American team	

Left Members of the expedition up Gaurishankar's West Face drop loads at Camp 1, a snow platform dug out of the small hanging glacier; the team included two Sherpas, Pertemba and Dorje (a co-leader with American, John Roskelley).

Big Mountain Climbs

Tawetse East Face with Bridwell and the ace Japanese climber, Naoe Sakashita. The West Pillar of Makulu, in virtual alpine style, was also Roskelley's. He gained renown as a careful, meticulous climber, with an eagle eye for detail, but could also be bold when it was needed – as he was to prove during the climb of Gaurishankar.

The co-leader of the expedition and one of its lead climbers, Sherpa Pertemba, had started off at a young age by carrying loads for the British Everest expedition in 1975. When he proved to be an able climber, he was rapidly promoted through the ranks to lead. He summitted the formidable southwest face route with Peter Boardman, on an expedition that was marred by the tragic death of Mick Burke. Pertemba followed this with the Gaurishankar climb, then immediately afterwards ascended Everest again with the 1979 German expedition. His third Everest summit was made in 1985 with a Norwegian team.

Sherpa Dorje was, as Pertemba had been in 1975, a young climber who wished to prove himself. His rapid acclimatization and his stoic determination soon found him in the vanguard of the climbers. He was technically skilled, and the logical choice of partner for a perfectionist such as Roskelley. Dorje ascended Everest for the first time in 1992, once again as part of an American expedition.

The climb

Briton Dennis Gray had led his men up the Bhote Kosi, a difficult and dangerous approach march, 15 years earlier. American climber Al Read chose the same route through the steep, densely forested high-altitude jungle. Little evidence remained of his predecessor's passage, except for the occasional remains of log or rope bridges over the deviously winding Chumal Chu.

Eventually, the team emerged on the Tseringma Col, which offered a stupendous view of the dramatic West Face of Gaurishankar on the opposite side of Tseringma Glacier. The original Northwest Ridge attempt route lay on the left – now in forbidden Tibetan territory, while the right-hand side was dominated by the steep and heavily corniced 3km (2-mile) Southwest Ridge, separated from the main summit by another, jagged, formidable-looking ridge. Their only option was the steeply angled 2800m (9200ft) West Face, a mass of ice,

rock and overhanging snow. Pertemba is alleged to have said: 'I think I see Gaurishankar and die.'

Base camp was made in the valley west of Tseringma Col, advance base on the glacier just north of the rib. Laboriously, supplies were carried in, while Roskelley, Pertemba, Dorje and Kim Schmitz worked out the intricacies of the slope.

Camp 1 was established at 5150m (16,900ft) on top of a small hanging glacier. Technical difficulties now began with a series of slippery slabs and friable ice runnels leading to the fluted rib. Before the climb, a decision had been taken to fix ropes over difficult sections (in the end, fixed ropes led virtually

all the way to the summit). This complicated the logistics, as vast amounts of rope and gear had to be transported up. Yet, considering the technical nature of the climb and limited experience of many support team members, it was the only sensible solution.

Camp 2 was established in a crevasse on the rib, out of the path of constant small avalanches. The next 350m (1150ft) of the rib took much time. Ropes had to be fixed all the way, due to the steep gradient and a constant peppering by ice and snow that threatened to sweep away any unattached climbers.

The next obstacle presented itself where the rib met a steep rock wall, impassable at this altitude. A

Above One of the expedition support climbers, Jim Morrissey, approaching Camp 1 via fixed ropes.

Opposite Dorje Sherpa making his way across steep and treacherous slopes towards the minute bivouac site of Camp 3.

Sherpas

Nowadays, Sherpas are well known for their involvement in high-altitude mountaineering. A small-boned people, they are tough and hardy, both mentally and physically. Although early Everest expeditions utilized Sherpas merely as porters, they are climbers in their own right. Today, they are pivotal in the success of many expeditions, and certainly hold the record for the number of high-altitude

long sideways traverse to the left seemed to be the only option, but the route was so steep and smooth in places that leaders Roskelley and Pertemba had to cross sections by tension traversing. Not only the ropes were tense; a 2000m (6500ft) abyss gaped below the climbers' feet! Via a steep yet climbable ice pitch they accessed a tiny platform where Camp 3 was established, and the tired climbers settled in.

The following day, Schmitz and Roskelley fixed ropes along a 100m (330ft) mixed stretch of near-vertical ice with small rock bands, many of which required advanced aiding techniques up to A3, quite a feat at altitudes close to 7000m (23,000ft).

Exhausted, Schmitz and Pertemba retreated, Dorje replacing them at Camp 3. In the summit attempt, Dorje and Roskelley approached the final passage leading up a 200m (650ft) hanging icefield

to a rock overhang. In the predawn darkness they managed to fit precarious pitons into the small crack that led through the void. Roskelley turned the overhang on these pitons at Grade A3 – making it, with the rest of this route, the hardest climb ever at this altitude (at the time). A last few metres of overhang, they progressed rapidly up the final snowfield, along the northwest ridge – and to the summit.

Descent was via a long series of airy abseils and careful descent down fixed ropes. The route still is a landmark of hard climbing although it was done siege-style, using plenty of fixed ropes and up-and-down movement by all the climbers, many of whom spent long periods above 6000m (19,700ft). It had some of the hardest aid pitches ever done above 6500m (21,300ft), and was the first ascent of a long sought-after major Himalayan peak.

ascents, both in the individual and group category. This fame is not obtained without risk – one-third of all high-altitude fatalities involve Sherpas.

Doubtlessly, the most famous Sherpa is Tenzing Norgay, who ascended Everest with Sir Edmund Hillary. Other notable names are Ang Rita, who has summitted Everest over seven times, and Pertemba.

Guiding and climbing often becomes a family tradition, with father and son (sometimes even grandfather) frequently taking part in the same expedition.

Above A victorious Dorje holds the Nepalese flag aloft on the summit of Gaurishankar.

Lightning Route – Changabang

Up the Shining Mountain at lightning speed

CHANGABANG IS A SPECTACULARLY BEAUTIFUL peak, located on the northwest wall of the famed Nanda Devi mountain sanctuary, in north India. *Nanda Devi* means 'bliss-giving goddess' – an apt name for the highest point in India, as the range often blocks the icy Himalayan blasts and hinders them from sweeping over the fertile plains below. The sanctuary has an interesting history of closures. In the mid-1960s it was declared off-limits after an avalanche had swept away a clandestine, nuclear-powered listening device, mounted high on Changabang's slopes, that was designed to monitor Chinese nuclear-missile activity in Tibet. Fears of radioactive pollution of the agriculturally important Rishi Ganga Gorge were, fortunately, unfounded. The sanctuary reopened for a few years from 1974, and there followed a number of new routes and first ascents, before its second closure in 1981. This time it was due to serious environmental concerns for the fragile, ecologically sensitive nature of the area. All those who have seen the gentle meadows below the imposing peaks agree that it is 'heaven on earth' and must be preserved.

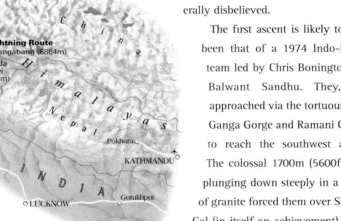

The mountain

The sanctuary was first penetrated as late as 1934, as access up the terrifyingly steep and very fast-running Rishi Ganga Gorge is extremely difficult. Eric Shipton (UK) and Bill Tilman (a naturalized Kenyan) fought their way into Nanda Devi to survey the peaks in the area, in the process climbing quite a few along the outer rim. Just two years later, in 1936, Tilman was back with Noel Odell and five other climbers, reaching the summit of Nanda Devi via the South Ridge – an effort regarded as 'the finest mountaineering achievement ever performed in the Himalayas' (Shipton), words that still stand true today.

Changabang has a reputation for difficult routes, and has guarded its summit carefully. W W Graham, a British surveyor of the area, claimed an ascent of Changabang and a number of other peaks nearby during a 1914 survey, but these are generally disbelieved.

The first ascent is likely to have been that of a 1974 Indo-British team led by Chris Bonington and Balwant Sandhu. They, too, approached via the tortuous Rishi Ganga Gorge and Ramani Glacier to reach the southwest aspect. The colossal 1700m (5600ft) face plunging down steeply in a sweep of granite forced them over Shipton Col (in itself an achievement) to the snow-covered Southeast Face and then to the knife-edged East Ridge, and finally the elusive summit.

Changabang is now more commonly known as the Shining Mountain, largely as a result of its fame through Peter Boardman's award-winning book of the same name. It lives up to this title with large blank walls of shining golden granite, capped with brilliant white snow. The Boardman-Tasker route on the West Face involved over 25 days of nonstop climbing, on rock of Grade VI/A2. It remains unrepeated to this day – a fitting tribute to the pair who opened it, and then disappeared without any trace

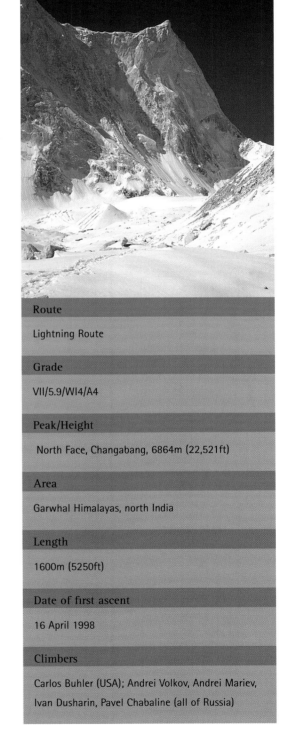

Route	
Lightning Route	
Grade	
VII/5.9/WI4/A4	
Peak/Height	
North Face, Changabang, 6864m (22,521ft)	
Area	
Garwhal Himalayas, north India	
Length	
1600m (5250ft)	
Date of first ascent	
16 April 1998	
Climbers	
Carlos Buhler (USA); Andrei Volkov, Andrei Mariev, Ivan Dusharin, Pavel Chabaline (all of Russia)	

Opposite Steve Sustad, of the UK, on superb ice on the North Face of Changabang. The incredibly steep wall does not retain snow for very long, making this, in effect, a mixed climb rather than a snow and ice big-wall route.

during their 1982 attempt on the unclimbed north-east face of Everest. The next significant attempt on Changabang was the Anglo-Polish assault of 1978, which opened up the South Buttress route. Wojtek Kurtyka and Krysztof Zurek, with Alex MacKintyre and John Porter (Grade VI/M5/A3) completed it in eight hectic days of full capsule-style climbing.

The route

The north side of Changabang was declared open in 1996, with an approach via the Bagini Glacier; no one, however, had ever been on this glacier.

In the summer of 1996, the secretary of the British Mountaineering Council, Roger Payne, and his wife, well-known climber Julie-Ann Clyma, attempted the steep and impressive North Face on its left-hand side. Unfortunately, bad weather forced them off, but not before they had reached high up on the iced-up slabs and corners of the face. Andy Perkins and Brendan Murphy, who were initially with the group, had been forced down sometime earlier due to illness.

1997 saw Roger, Julie-Ann and Brendan back, with Mick Fowler, Steve Sustad and Andy Cave (all of the UK). Roger and Julie-Ann tried their original

line, while the other four attempted a route in the middle of the left-hand buttress, climbing alpine-style in two independent pairs. They met with heavy snowfalls, and battled the deep, crumbly snow and low temperatures until the face was so steep that only hard ice remained. The team of four split into two, and all summitted, Andy and Brendan on 1 June, the other two a day later. On the descent, Steve slipped; both he and Mick fell 65m (200ft) before Steve hit a rock, sustaining chest injuries, but his fall had saved them. Andy and Brendan joined in to lower him off. Tragically, an avalanche swept Brendan off his stance while he was setting pegs for a lowering traverse; his body was never recovered. Payne and Clyma had sat out 10 days of storms high on the face before abseiling down. They only learned of Murphy's tragic death back at base camp.

At this point in a history of impenetrability, a US-Russian team made its appearance. American Carlos Buhler had heard the tale of the previous

group's successful attempt and horrifying tragedy and began to enquire about routes to the right. The realization that it was possible but would involve a big-wall route was sobering – it meant true big-wall climbing at high altitude.

The climbers

Buhler is a prolific climber, whose achievements include sport and traditional climbs in the USA, as well as routes in the Himalayas and other major ranges. Among his exploits is a difficult new route on the central rib of Everest's Southwest Face in 1983. In 1996 he joined the Russian team (listed below) on the north ridge of K2. With the same group he successfully climbed the huge and complex Diamir Face of Nanga Parbat in late 1996.

Ivan Dusharin, Andrei Mariev, Pavel Chabaline and Andrei Volkov built up considerable experience climbing together in the Pamirs. All but Pavel were part of the highly successful US-Soviet Détente

Above The North Face of Changabang looms over Steve Sustad as he makes his way up a steep icefield.

Opposite top Approaching the final pitches on the rock tower which leads up to the summit ridge of Changabang.

Opposite bottom The last photograph of Brendan Murphy (right) before he was tragically swept away by an avalanche.

expedition of K2 in 1996. Their subsequent success on the notorious Nanga Parbat inspired them to join Carlos Buhler on the technically challenging North Face of Changabang. Pavel, one of the most experienced and highly regarded Russian names in big-wall and aid-climbing, was included as well.

The climb

Studying the wall for the first time, the men were staggered by the immensity of the 1600m (5250ft) of ice-plastered golden granite. They spent time watching the mountain and listening to it, to pinpoint the maximum avalanche and stonefall times. After days of survey and line fixing on the four lower ice pitches they decided to depart. Just then a major storm moved in. Sitting it out nervously, aware that advance base camp was uncomfortably close to the face and its massive avalanche potential, they used this time to thrash out basic philosophical differences between the American and Russian approaches. Buhler believed in a democratic way that allowed climbers to take it in turns to pioneer sections of the route, while the Russians were motivated by the team approach, which dictated that fulfilment of a common goal was more important than individual glory. The result was a clever compromise that encouraged each member to choose his role. From support to load carrying, load hauling, lead climber, deputy lead climber, belayer-in-chief and cook…each climber knew his function (and the roles became increasingly fixed as the climb progressed).

Bad conditions persisted, and the team decided to make its way down one night for a spell of rest on the base camp meadow. In chest-deep snow, the two-hour trip lasted over eight hours. Perhaps as a consequence of this long, late-night foray, Buhler developed bronchitis, which excluded him from setting up the first few pitches and reduced his influence in establishing the climbing pattern.

A week later, on 10 May, they were fixing ropes up the next six pitches, now increasingly consisting of mixed rock and ice. Once these were in place, the first 'hell day' arrived: hauling hundreds of kilograms of supplies up to the high point for a hanging bivouac – three Russians crammed into a small, one-man bivvy tent. Buhler was involved in the logistics of supplying the front-leading team, Chabaline and Volkov, when an inventory of the

fuel supply surprised him. What had looked like enough fuel for a month turned out to be mostly of the 110-proof alcohol variety – good for warming up the body on long, cold nights, but not for stoves!

Their pattern was: climb, belay, sort, sleep. Every few days were haul days – a 15kg (33 lb) sack on the back, a 25kg (55 lb) haul bag clipped to the leg loops of the harness, endless jumaring up a single, slowly fraying 9mm fixed rope…

Long days followed, sections of free-climbing on sparse protection interspersed with pitches of aid-climbing. The mountain face received virtually no sun, temperatures were low and cracks often filled

with ice, and had to be chipped to accept protection or create handholds. Falling stones, ice and small avalanches kept reminding the team that an accident would be disastrous. Pure ice sections offered little respite – they were hard as steel and brittle like glass. Hypothermia was a constant danger, particularly for the belayers who had to remain stationary for hours.

Then, the final ridge! Darkness prevented traverse to the summit and the team descended to the bivouac point for another uncomfortable night. When the snow stopped the next morning, they raced up the fixed ropes to the long-awaited summit. 'For a few moments we were free from the burden of the wall. It occurred to me that it was the first time I had been able to stand on something in over two weeks.' (Buhler, 1999) After summitting, they retraced their steps carefully, two days of continuous rappelling and cleaning, to reach safety at the base of the wall.

At 1600m (5250ft), the Lightning Route with its unimaginable grades of VII/5.9/WI4/A4 is a truly modernistic route, combining Himalayan capsule-style approaches with committing free- and aid-climbing up soaring granite crack and friction climbs. The route took 21 days from its start at the base to the completion of the many abseils down.

South Face – Lhotse

Fact or fiction?

LHOTSE, AT 8516M (27,941FT), IS THE FOURTH highest of the 8000m (26,000ft) peaks. Despite its position near the top of the list, it is to some extent a 'forgotten 8000', largely because it stands in the shadow (literally) of Mt Everest, which is 337m (1105ft) higher. The standard Northwest Face route up Lhotse is the same as Everest's normal South Face route up to the 7300m (23,950ft) mark, the South Col. Lhotse was first climbed via this route by E Reiss and F Luchsinger in 1956.

It is Lhotse's South Face, however, that presents a problem. The formidable wall of rock, snow and ice towers 3500m (11,500ft) over its approach glaciers. From 1972 (which saw the first serious attempt) to 1990, the South Face repelled 13 separate assaults and was dubbed 'the last great problem of the Himalayas' and 'problem for the year 2000' by Reinhold Messner. It is an uncompromisingly steep wall, ravaged by avalanches and broken by a characteristic 'yellow band' of rock above 8000m (26,000ft) – the same layer that frequently poses problems on many Everest routes. The South Face had already claimed the lives of Jerzy Kukuczka (see also p151), who fell from the summit ridge in 1989; fellow Pole, Rafal Holda, who had joined him on a previous attempt in 1985; and the first soloist, Jaeger. Among the parties whose repeated summit attempts had been repelled were those of Reinhold Messner, the first climber to conquer all 14 of the 8000m (26,000ft) peaks, and Krysztof Wielicki, regarded as one of Poland's toughest climbers.

The route

Most of the parties who had attempted the route since the early 1970s followed a line from right to left, up the huge central spur that breaks the face. The South Face of Lhotse appears to offer no respite from avalanches and rockfalls, no matter where one turns, and this route had always seemed to be the safest choice. The top of the spur poses the first of a number of major technical problems: does one turn left up a steepening (but safer) rockband, or right across a terrifyingly exposed central gully that acts as an avalanche channel for the vast bowl of the face?

Yugoslav Ales Kunaver and his team explored the vast face via the middle spur in 1981. Four years later, the French climbers Michel Fauquet and Vincent Fine headed in, alpine-style, and broke right at about halfway up the rib onto a series of smaller ones. They made it to 7400m (24,300ft) without incident, then retreated due to bad weather. Later, Yugoslav Tom Césen's successful climb of 1990 took this breakaway route; he followed a zigzag ascent line of the lower face, up to the central spur, which was ascended on the west flank to where a series of smaller spurs, adjacent to it, opened a pathway across to (relative) shelter under the large triangular wall. A further fragile and precarious ice section via the funnel at the base of the large snowfield led onto this field, which is taken on its western side to the notorious yellow band. A few hundred metres of steep, mixed rock, ice and shale

Route	
South Face of Lhotse	
Grade	
ED+	
Peak/Height	
Lhotse, 8516m (27,941ft)	
Area	
Himalayas, East Nepal	
Length	
3500m (11,500ft)	
Date of first ascent	
April 1990	
Climber	
Tomo Césen (Slovenia)	

Left Lhotse's immense South Face, in the East Nepalese Himalayas, rises almost vertically for a staggering 3500m (11,500ft) from the head of the valley to the elusive summit pyramid.

lead to a gradually easing ramp to the summit. Descent was via mostly the same line, with more direct abseils down the initial rock band.

The climber

Tomo Césen was born in Kranj, Slovenia (then Yugoslavia), in 1959, where he still lives with his wife and two sons. A small village near the borders of Italy and Austria, Kranj lies in the mountainous area near Triglav, which has faces of up to 1000m (3300ft) high. Tomo soon became interested in climbing, and by the age of 18 he had become a member of the elite club of top Yugoslav alpinists. Struggling against the relative poverty common among Eastern-bloc climbers under the communist regime, he still managed to visit the Alps and a number of other world climbing areas, where he quickly and quietly made his mark by climbing the hardest routes as fast as possible – frequently solo.

These climbing exploits included the Bonatti Pillar on the Petit Dru, the Gabarrou Couloir on Mt Blanc de Tacul, the North Face of Les Droites, North Face of Peak Communism (7563m; 24,814ft), and West Summit of Kangchenjunga. Césen first drew major public attention however, when, following unsuccessful attempts on the 'trilogy' by Christofe Profit and Eric Escoffier, he climbed the Eiger North Face, the Grandes Jorasses via the Shroud, and the Matterhorn, all within a week, solo and in winter. In typical fashion Césen, a shy, reserved man, eschewed the ensuing publicity.

A string of sensational solo feats followed: No Siesta, a 1200m (4000ft), 90-degree ice route on the Grandes Jorasses, the 8047m (26,402ft) Broad Peak, and in 1986, K2 to a height of 8150m (26,750ft). Just below the summit he wisely retreated in the face of the storm that cost so many lives that year. In 1989 he did Modern Times in under seven hours, a desperately hard (6c/5.11a) rock route on Marmolada's South Face. In April of that year, he stunned the climbing fraternity with yet another innovative

solo attempt: he climbed the North Face of Jannu (7710m; 25,296ft) in the Himalayas, in 23 hours nonstop. The route, with its 2800m (9200ft) of rock and ice faces angled at up to 90 degrees, was considered the most difficult climb ever achieved.

'Once I'd started up the Shadow Buttress on Jannu, I realized how right I was to start off alone. This allowed me rapid progress, and the power to take important decisions to get me out alive. You have to know how to move really, really fast! From above a certain height, considering the commitment and paucity of equipment, it was impossible for me to descend. So I had to go on and up in the right direction. It's just as well I have good intuition.' (Tomo Césen, in an interview by Claude Rémy)

The climb

With Jannu under his belt, Césen felt ready to solo Lhotse. Never leaving anything to chance, Césen's methodical preparation involves the study of a mountain from every possible angle using photographs and reconnaissance trips. He obtained photos of Lhotse from Ales Kunaver, who had attempted it in 1981. Just prior to Ales's expedition, two Yugoslav climbers had been sent to base camp to mark every avalanche on one of the photos. In 1987, Césen studied these pictures and the actual face from Lhotse Shar. Slowly, he accumulated the necessary information, until he was in a position to start preparing himself, physically and psychologically.

On the afternoon of 22 April, Tomo set out with minimal bivouac gear, 100m (330ft) of 6mm rope, and determination. He moved quickly up the rib into the gathering darkness, and by 06:00 the next morning was at 7500m (24,600ft) for his first bivouac, having bypassed most of the avalanche danger in the cold of night. He repeated this pattern, starting out again at 17:00 to move rapidly into the gorge of the giant couloir. In his words, 'The desire to climb fast here was greater than my body's capacity to respond.' Climbing continuously through the snowfield, he rapidly reached the top rockband in the darkness of evening, for his second long, sleepless bivouac at 8200m (26,900ft).

The next morning dawned clear, bright and promising. Tomo left most of his bivouac gear behind, committing himself to the race for the top. The last few hundred metres consisted of snow-and-ice-plastered rock that would have been easy at alpine altitudes, but was desperately hard in the thin, mind-dulling air at 8000m (26,000ft).

Slowly he moved upwards, metres at a time, when the weather changed and it began to snow. On the crest of the ridge a strong wind sprang up. Finally, at 02:20, Tomo trudged up the small snow slope beyond a dip on the ridge to find himself on the summit of Lhotse.

Guided by experience, Césen started down immediately, despite his weariness, retracing his steps to 7800m (25,600ft), well below his last bivouac. From there he abseiled down the 'giant triangle' of rock, the only path relatively safe from the constant avalanches. By the time he had reached the bottom of this wall, the snow was falling thick and fast, cutting off all visibility. Césen was forced to bivouac at 7300m (23,900ft), unseen avalanches thundering down around him. At around midnight stars appeared, and he decided to move down fast while weather and avalanches held off. Constantly aware of the tons of unstable snow and ice suspended above his head and remembering the fellow climbers who had lost their lives in just such situations (two in virtually the same spot), he traversed around the face, seeking a way down in the tiny circle of light cast by his fading headlamp.

At 08:00 he realized he was down, and could finally relax. 'I found it difficult to think, to summon any feelings. I know, though, that Lhotse took part of my soul.' (Césen, quoted in *Mountain* 134)

The controversy

Controversy is nothing new in the competitive world of mountaineering. Did Mallory make it up Everest? Did Cesare Maestri climb Cerro Torre along the North Face route that was subsequently found to be impregnable? Was Herman Buhl really on top of Nanga Parbat? And did Césen summit Lhotse? There are no concrete answers to these questions. Often, the only claim lies in the word of the climber.

After the Lhotse solo, Césen was acclaimed and fêted by the climbing establishment. Soon, however, various famous climbers who had initially supported him, joined the ranks of those who had had serious doubts right from the start, and his ascent was called into question. Unfortunately, there was no proof – other than Tomo Césen's word.

Doubt and disbelief were fuelled largely by the sheer difficulty of the route. If so many great climbers had failed before, why should he have succeeded? Yet, his record of solo ascents was truly awesome. Or was it?

It was not long before those claims, too, were widely questioned. The odds were not in Tomo Césen's favour: in many cases, he had told no-one of his successful solo climbs for weeks afterwards. His apparent disinterest in the raucous publicity circus that normally surrounds any astounding climbing feat had become a weapon against him.

When the Swiss Rémy brothers proposed an unsuspecting Césen for inclusion in the elite Groupe de Haute Montagne (GHM), French members blocked his entry. This prompted renowned French alpinist and GHM member, Pierre Beghin, to come out in Tomo's support. 'I have always believed that one of the golden rules of alpinism was respect for the word of others. Everyone is presumed innocent until found guilty. Will we in future have to produce proof of all our achievements? If we, as alpinists, allow suspicion to intrude amongst ourselves, then we lose part of our soul.'

Staunch support from Beghin, Profit and Escoffier, among others, finally did see Césen admitted to the GHM, but the controversy rages on, fuelled by astute comments from climbers of undeniable stature. Their negative opinions, however, are balanced by positive ones coming from the equally august ranks of the 'opposing camp'. In the final analysis, all comes down to personal opinion. As for the truth, only Césen holds that key. What cannot be denied is that he is an extraordinarily good climber with impressive ascents to his name.

Whether Tomo Césen really did climb the South Face of Lhotse, or not, the very thought that it might be done has served to inspire countless others to try, thereby rapidly raising the standards of extreme alpinism at altitude.

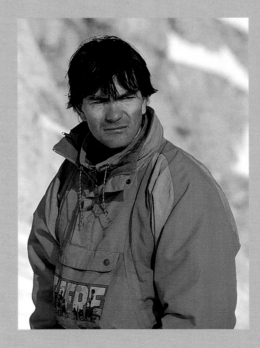

Above Césen, confident and at home on the sandstone cliffs of his native Slovenia.
Left A contemplative Tomo Césen. Hero or fraud?
Opposite top Easier ground in the European Alps.
Opposite bottom Lhotse's long west ridge runs from Nuptse on the far left to Lhotse with its plume of cloud on the right.

Polish Route – K2

The mountain of mountains

K2 IS THE SECOND HIGHEST PEAK IN THE world. It lies in splendid isolation deep in the Upper Karakorum, in the heart of the wild mountain range. Unlike most of the other high peaks, K2 has no local name, as it is invisible from any habitation. Initially, it was simply named 'K', as one of the Karakorum peaks, during the first British Indian survey of 1856. The name has stuck, lending it a well-deserved air of mystery.

Many unsuccessful attempts and countless fatalities ushered in the first ascent in 1954. A big team of Italian climbers under the leadership of Professor Ardito Desio made their way up K2 via the Abruzzi Spur (named after the Duke of Abruzzi who pioneered the route in 1909, reaching 6250m/20,500ft). Two of them, Lino Lacedelli and Achille Compagnoni, made it to the top, despite having run out of oxygen. In a precarious descent, both very nearly lost their lives when a cornice collapsed. After this first full ascent, the K2 gained a macabre reputation by repulsing all further efforts, while continuing to claim the lives of those who dared. It retained its ominous aura until 1977, when a massive 42-person expedition successfully placed six Japanese and one Pakistani climber on the summit. Still today, K2 is regarded as probably the most formidable of all 8000m (26,000ft) peaks. Reinhold Messner, the widely respected and highly experienced guru of Himalayan climbing, has justifiably called it the hardest mountain in the world.

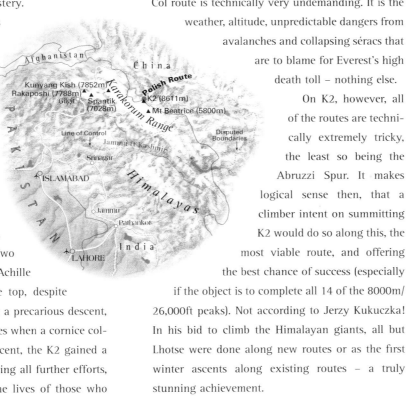

The route

K2's notoriety is not without reason. There is no easy route up, no 'tourist track' that guides can use to take clients to the summit in relative safety. Although the same can, to some extent, be said for most high mountains, one only has to look at the number of 'clients' who have been guided to the summit of Everest to realize that its standard South Col route is technically very undemanding. It is the weather, altitude, unpredictable dangers from avalanches and collapsing séracs that are to blame for Everest's high death toll – nothing else.

On K2, however, all of the routes are technically extremely tricky, the least so being the Abruzzi Spur. It makes logical sense then, that a climber intent on summitting K2 would do so along this, the most viable route, and offering the best chance of success (especially if the object is to complete all 14 of the 8000m/ 26,000ft peaks). Not according to Jerzy Kukuczka! In his bid to climb the Himalayan giants, all but Lhotse were done along new routes or as the first winter ascents along existing routes – a truly stunning achievement.

The route Kukuczka chose on K2 was a new one on the steep South Face, one that led to extremely difficult climbing. The top section, in particular, was technically demanding, as it culminates in the treacherous exposed Hockey Stick Gulley and a forbidding rock barrier, just before moving onto an easy ridge that joins the final few metres of the Abruzzi Spur to the summit.

Route	
Polish Route	
Grade	
ED+	
Peak/Height	
South Face, K2, 8611m (28,253ft)	
Area	
Central (Greater) Karakorum, Pakistan	
Length	
3000m (10,000ft)	
Date of first ascent	
July 1986	
Climbers	
Jerzy Kukuczka, Tadeus Piotrowski (both of Poland)	

Opposite Tiredness shows on the face of the top climber in this picture taken on the North Ridge. Sadly, pictures of the Polish South Face route established by Kukuczka and Piotrowski are not available – both climbers are deceased.

The climbers

Pole Jerzy Kukuczka was a truly amazing person. Mild-mannered and unassuming, he did not resemble a climber let alone an expert of extreme Himalayan conditions. Yet, he had admirable inner strength, developed during a harsh childhood in then-communist Poland. His friend and climbing partner, Wojtek Kurtyka, who, like Jerzy, is regarded as one of Poland's greatest climbers, said, 'Polish kids were taught to be tough. If you were not tough, you were weak and were a bad boy. In Poland ... we had to always be ready for another uprising, another hard struggle. This attitude was shifted to the mountains, so that a Polish climber would think three times before coming down.' (*Beyond Risk, Conversations with Climbers*)

Polish climbers have earned a justified reputation in Himalayan and Alpine climbing, with many extreme routes to their credit, but Kukuczka was the embodiment of the Silesian toughness.

He started climbing as a schoolboy in 1965, and soon progressed from the short rock routes of the Beskid mountains to alpine-scale climbs in the Tatra. This was followed by expeditions to Alaska, the Hindu Kush and, eventually, a dream realized in the real Himalayas – Nanga Parbat in 1977.

In 1979, he started on his '14 peaks' with the Northwest Face of Lhotse, finishing it with his ascent of Shisha Pangma in 1987. During his climbing career, five of his partners died while accompanying him. This resulted in a somewhat infamous reputation, although his survival when

others perished is, perhaps, even more of a tribute to his own skill and strength, as well as – of his own admission – to a large slice of luck.

Lhotse was the only 'repeat route' on his quest to summit the 14 giants; the others were conquered along new lines or under different circumstances. In some ways, this made Lhotse seem incomplete to Jerzy, and he returned to attempt the unclimbed South Face route in 1985, and again in 1989. It was on this occasion that, high up on the face, after climbing a long way without finding any form of protection, he slipped and fell onto a 6mm rope. It broke and Jerzy plummeted to his death.

Tadek (Tadeus) Piotrowski, a man of immense physical power and resilience, was another one of Poland's highly regarded climbers. He had done

numerous first winter ascents in the Tatra, the Alps and Norway, had been on the first winter ascent of the 7000m (22,970ft) Noshaq in 1973, and taken part in the 1974 ascent of Lhotse, in which Polish climber, Latallo, died. Tadeus was blamed for this tragedy although it had clearly not been anyone's fault. He left climbing for a number of years to write mountaineering books, but could not resist a call by Munich-based expedition organizer, Dr Karl Herrligkoffer, to accompany Kukuczka on K2.

The Expedition

Jerzy preferred to tackle his climbs alpine-style, or at least in a small group. When he was invited to join a large international expedition, he had serious doubts until three important factors finally

decided the issue. Firstly, finding the funds for an intricate expedition such as this presented a major headache in cash-strapped Poland. His 14-peak schedule had already been delayed for quite some time and, although he was ostensibly not taking it too seriously, he was still racing German climber Reinhold Messner to be the first to finish. Messner, who had virtually unlimited funds at his disposal, was very clearly in a superior position. (Eventually, Messner did go on to be the first person to climb all 14 of the 8000m/26,250ft Himalayan giants – a truly magnificent achievement, justly deserved.)

Jerzy realized that personal costs on this expedition would be minor, while allowing him to attempt the new route he dreamed of.

The second reason was Tadeus Piotrowski, who had invited him along. Not only was Tadeus his friend, he was also an experienced mountaineer and excellent partner, whom he respected immensely. With a man like him, Jerzy realized, he would have a very good chance at the summit.

The third factor was Dr Karl Herrligkoffer, renowned as a superb expedition organizer. He ran his many Himalayan expeditions extremely well,

Opposite A cheerful climber, despite his precariously positioned tent, during the North Ridge expedition of 1996.
Above The steep East Face of K2 repulsed a 1989 Austrian expedition, whose ladder can be seen here.

After a brief foray back to the base camp, Jerzy, Tadek and the German guide, Toni Freudig, set off. They moved up to 6400m (21,000ft), the high point Jerzy and Wojtek Kurtyka had reached on a recce two years before. The key to the route now lay ahead – the traverse under a colossal and unstable sérac, pieces of which were falling off constantly.

When Toni began feeling unwell, Tadek and Jerzy left him in his tent and raced across beneath the sérac at 04:00, well before the sun could loosen any ice above. Fixing ropes up a steep arête they reached nearly 7000m (23,000ft). When the pair scurried down again that night, Toni decided to return to base. This left them free to move alpine-style, tent and all, back up the fixed ropes and onto a tiny platform of snow at 7200m (23,600ft). It began to snow in earnest, forcing the pair to retreat to base camp the next day, leaving their tent in place, hooked to a single piton.

Ten days later the sun finally reappeared, and after another few days they decided the snow had settled enough to be safe. Two days later they were at their previous camp site, which had to be dug out of hard snow. The following day brought them to the curved Hockey Stick Gully and a precarious bivouac at 7800m (25,600ft). At 8200m (26,900ft) their progress was barred by a 100m (330ft) rockband. At this altitude and with only a few nuts and pitons for protection, it took Jerzy a full day to climb the crux 30m (100ft) of Grade V+ rock. Snow again began to fall and the pair knew that the next day was either summit, or back.

At the bivouac, Jerzy let their single precious gas canister fall into the depths below. This meant

and allowed food and equipment luxuries that Polish climbers could only dream of. In his book, *My Vertical World*, Kukuczka gives an entertaining account of being a Polish climber on an affluent Western expedition. Unlimited food, unlimited hot water at base camp, helicopter mail flights, freeze-dried, instant sumptuous meals, and superior equipment. The only downside, in his opinion, was that the other climbers on this trip were soft, and lacked the drive to push new routes.

Despite the fact that Herrligkoffer had managed to obtain a permit for new routes on Broad Peak and the South Face of K2, the Swiss and German members of the expedition all opted for the standard route on Broad Peak or the Abruzzi Spur. All Kukuczka wanted, however, was a chance to go the South Face route – with or without the others. In the face of the team's deplorable lack of spirit, he had already decided to compromise his attitude to large expeditions when a surprising turn of events ensured that he would get his chance at an alpine-style approach, anyway. Herrligkoffer, a

supporter of large, siege-style attempts, threw his support behind Kukuczka's lightweight do-or-die suggestion and, in a somewhat dictatorial fashion, ordered the rest of the climbers to comply. This resulted in some interesting political moments, but no real friction ensued.

The climb

Early in July 1986, Jerzy Kukuczka, Tadek Piotrowski, three Swiss and one German guide left base camp for the South Face route. Several days of plodding through fresh, deep snow eventually brought the group to 6000m (19,700ft) and the chosen site for Camp 1. Two of the Swiss apprehensively scanned the surrounding slopes and opted to go back down first thing the next day, rather than chance what they felt were imminent avalanches or sérac falls. Early the following morning, Jerzy fell through a cornice on the ridge (luckily he had already roped up to Tadek). This swiftly settled things for the third Swiss climber, who decided to descend as well.

Above A colossal avalanche thunders down from the massive overhanging séracs on K2.

Right A climber trudges upwards over the broken ground of the relentless upper slopes of K2.

no more drinks of any kind, a serious position to be in when one considers that the body needs a good deal of liquid in the rarefied, dry air above 8000m (26,000ft). Climbing in a dehydrated state was going to make things that much harder.

They decided to go for the summit without rucksacks, taking only climbing gear and a minimal amount of emergency equipment. From then on, any mistake could cost them their lives. After swiftly moving up the ropes they had fixed before, they managed to finish the rockband by 15:00, in mist and snow. A much easier ridge now led to the Abruzzi Spur and the summit. The pair moved on, visibility dropping all the time.

Three hours later they still had not reached the summit and became concerned, but after a final sérac, there it was. Victory! Tadek's first 8000m (26,000ft) summit and Jerzy's 11th, attained by the hardest route ever climbed on the peak.

By now darkness had fallen. As they reached their stash of emergency gear at the top of the rockband, Jerzy, tired and cold, dropped the only torch battery and they had no choice but to bivouac, digging a shallow cave to huddle in.

The morning brought no improvement in visibility. Mist and blinding snow hid all features from view. The climbers were trapped above 8000m – cold, hungry, tired and dehydrated in a white world. Descent by the route they had come was impossible; they had to climb down the steep Abruzzi Spur, unknown to either of them. Depending only on the memory of photographs and others' accounts, they moved downward, abseiling off precarious rock spikes and down-climbing the iced-up

snow. By nightfall they found themselves below the steep upper reaches, and dug another shallow cave. This was their fourth night at high altitude, their energy was severely depleted, the mental strain was intense and they were feeling increasingly confused.

Dawn brought some relief in a lessening of the snow and mist. Jerzy set off to find the easiest route, reminding Tadek to bring the rope for steep sections ahead. When Tadek finally caught up with him, he had left the rope behind. Again the slope

steepened. The pair were forced to down-climb, relying on their axes and crampon points. Then Jerzy heard a shout, and saw Tadek's crampons fly down at him, one after the other. Finding himself suddenly without vital footing, the stricken Tadek gave a scream, then plunged off the face, knocking into a precariously balanced Jerzy. He disappeared over a huge cliff 100m (330ft) below. No trace of Piotrowski's body has ever been found.

Kukuczka made it to tents left by an Austrian group, where he unsuccessfully attempted to make radio contact with others. The following day he found his way to a Korean expedition, who looked after him until he could venture back to base camp with his news. Once again, K2 had exacted its heavy toll. It had granted him a successful summit, but taken a valued friend and companion.

During this 1986 climbing season, 13 other mountaineers died on K2, including two more Poles, Dobroslawa Wolf and Wojtek Wroz.

Above An all-too-common occurrence on K2 – a dead climber is brought down from the mountain.
Left Looking southwards from the summit of K2; Broad Peak is on the right, Gasherbrum 2, 3 and 4 behind it.

Abseil: means of descending a rope safely; speed is controlled by friction of the rope around the body, or an abseil device. Also known as rappel.

ACU (ACD): Active Camming Unit (or device); protection device – spring-loaded metal cams that expand and 'bite' into the rock under tension.

Aid climbing: the climber relies on protection equipment (pegs, nuts, ACUs, and others) for upward progression; is also known as artificial climbing.

Alpine-style: alpine climbing on the world's great mountain ranges (includes glacier or snow travel on the higher mountains, and the ascent of a peak); the route is ascended in one push, without fixed ropes and numerous heavily stocked subcamps.

Arête: narrow ridge of rock, ice or snow; on smaller cliffs it is a narrow, steep ridge of rock.

Ascender: mechanical device used to ascend a rope; usually used in pairs (*see* Jumar).

Base jump: extreme parachute jump off a high mountain or building (illegal).

Bat hook: *see* Skyhook.

Belay: system (anchor, belayer and belay device or method) used to break a fall by using a rope. To belay is to hold a rope in such a way as to be able to arrest a fall; person being held is the 'belayed'.

Big wall climb: technically demanding route; not every pitch need be 'climbed' by each climber, mechanical ascenders are often used by the second climber to follow the leader.

Bivouac: overnight position without a tent; a climber often spends it hanging from a rock, minute ledge, or tiny crack.

Bolt: metal expansion device, fastened into predrilled hole in the rock; used for belays or running protection.

Bong: large metal wedge or tube used as protection in a crack in the rock face.

Bouldering: unroped climbing on small rock faces, including climbing walls and buildings.

Camming device: *see* ACU.

Carabiner (crab): metal snap ring that opens on one side (gate); used to attach protection devices to slings or ropes.

Chimney: large crack that can accommodate a climber, feet on one side, back on opposite wall; climbed by 'wedging' up.

Classic route: a superb climb with an outstanding reputation due to factors such as location, history, or an elegant line; can be any climbing grade.

Copperheads: copper lumps on wire loops; bashed into rock seams to afford tenuous points of aid, or marginal protection; used mainly in aid climbing.

Couloir: snow-filled gully.

Crampons: metal frames with sharp spikes that are attached to rigid climbing boots; these provide vital purchase on steep snow or ice slopes.

Crux: most difficult section or move of a climb.

Dihedral: *see* open-book corner.

Dry-tooling: ice axes torqued into cracks or resting on small protruberances (as opposed to embedding them in ice); used for upwards movement.

Etrier: multiloop sling to stand in; used in aid climbing.

Free-soling: climbing alone without a rope.

Grigri: an auto-locking device used for belaying and abseiling; also used by solo climbers.

Jug: large hold on a rock.

Jugging: ascending a rope using mechanical ascenders (*see* Jumar).

Jumar: original make of metal-toothed ascending device that clamps onto a rope; technique of ascending ropes by using similar ascenders.

Lead-out: long section covered by the climbing leader without being able to place any protection gear whatsoever.

Mantelshelf: technical move to overcome a high step, or get onto a ledge; the arms are used to press upwards, until a foot can be swung onto the ledge.

Mixed route: usually a climbing route that involves both rock- and snow- or ice-climbing techniques to complete.

Natural gear: protection placed by the leading climber and removed by the second, such as nuts and ACUs (not predrilled bolts or pegs).

Nut: name for a metal wedge, or chock, designed to offer protection; used in cracks.

Off-width: crack in the rock that is too small to accommodate the body (*see* Chimney), but too large to allow for a convenient hand or foot jam; usually awkward to climb.

On-sight: to lead a climb flawlessly for the first time, without prior knowledge of the route or the moves involved.

Open-book corner: a large, open-angled corner on a rock face.

Peg: *see* Piton.

Pitch: section of rock, snow or ice that is climbed between major belay points; often a pitch stops at a suitable stance or anchor point.

Piton (peg or pin): metal spike with an attachment eye for a carabiner; it is hammered into crevices for use as protection.

Portaledge: collapsible, reinforced stretcher used on hanging bivouacs or as belay ledge, mostly on big wall climbs.

Protection: nylon slings, hangers, or metal devices (nuts, chocks, hexes, stoppers, and ACUs) fixed into the rock; used to stop a climber from falling too far, or to anchor climbers or ropes to belay points.

Prusik: small piece of strong cord specially tied around a rope, used as a means of ascending a rope (in place of a jumar); action of ascending a rope by using this device.

Rappel (rap): *see* Abseil.

Redpointing: a climbing style (usually only featured in sport climbing)

that allows any amount and form of practice and preparation of the route, providing that the climb is finally led without weighting the runners.

Runner: combination of protection devices e.g. a sling and carabiner used to stop a fall.

Sérac: a pinnacle, tower or large block of ice; usually found on glaciers or at the head of valleys.

Skyhook (bat hook): a small, curved metal hook that is used to latch onto tiny rock flakes, or fit in small cracks for protection; it is usually used in aid climbing.

Slab: any large, off-vertically inclined mass of rock, often quite featureless and offering little protection; best climbed with balance techniques.

Sustained: the term used for a route with a continuous, high level of difficulty that demands constant concentration.

Technical: refers to climbing routes that have complex and difficult advanced moves requiring much skill and careful thought, concentration as well as precision technique.

Traditional climbing: also called natural-gear, trad and adventure climbing; the climber makes use only of natural features in the rock to place protection gear such as slings, nuts, cams; no drilled-in bolts are used at all.

Top-rope: climbing a pitch without leading it; the safety rope is attached to the climber from above.

Topo: semi-pictorial diagram to illustrate the line of a route.

Top out: finish climb or pitch.

Torque: twisting a piece of equipment, such as an ice axe (or part of one's body) so that it wedges tightly in a crack.

Tyrolean traverse: a way of crossing a deep gap by means of a rope that has been tensioned between two points on either side of the drop. The climber pulls him- or herself along the rope from one side to the other. This technique gets its name from the Austrian Tyrol region, where the method originated.

UIAGM: *Union Internationale des Associations des Guides des Montagnes*, the European international guiding body.

Left Swiss climber Kim Schmitz on the Grand Ice Traverse leading to the Camp 3 bivouac on the West Face of Gaurishankar.

ROCK CLIMBING GRADING SYSTEMS

UIAA	FRANCE	USA	BRITAIN (TECHNICAL)	BRITAIN (SEVERITY)	AUSTRALIA/NZ SOUTH AFRICA	GERMANY
I	1	5.2		Moderate	9	I
II	2	5		Difficult	10	II
III	3	5.4		Very Difficult	11	III
IV	4	5.5	4a	Severe (S)	12	IV
V-					13	V
V		5.6	4b	Very Severe	14	VI
V+	5	5.7	4c		15	VIIa
VI-		5.8	5a	Hard VS	16/17	VIIb
VI	6a	5.9		E1	18	
VI+	6a+	5.10a/b	5b		19	VIIc
VII-	6b	5.10c/d		E2	20	VIIIa
VII	6b+	5.11a	5c		21	VIIIb
VII+	6c	5.11b		E3	22	VIIIc
VIII-	6c+	5.11c	6a		23	IXa
VIII	7a/7a+	5.11c		E4	25	IXb
VIII+	7b	5.12a/b	6b		26	IXc
IX-	7b+/7c	5.12c		E5	27	Xa
IX	7c+	5.12d			28	Xb
IX+	8a	5.13a	6c		29	Xc
X-	8a+	5.13b		E6	30	
X	8b	5.13c/d	7a		31	
X+	8b+	5.14a		E7	32	
XI-	8c	5.14b	7b		33	
XI	8c+	5.14c	7c	E8/9	34	
XI+	9a	5.14d	8a	E9	35/36	

NOTE: Grading systems are open-ended. The grades shown here reflect the highest current grades at the time of compilation. Direct comparison between two adjacent climbs can be difficult, let alone comparing grades between different countries or differing types of climbing – the area and the nationality of the climbers help one identify which grading system is in use! The grade of a climb is given by the opening party, and eventually accepted by consensus of the climbing community, but will always be the subject of much debate.

Alpine grades
Alpine-type routes (and many mixed and big wall routes) are given an overall 'difficulty of route' grade. Climbers may use one of a number of systems: the French scale, from F – *facile* (easy), via PD – *peu difficile* (moderately difficult), AD, D, TD to ED – *extrèmement difficile* (extremely difficult); the UIAA scale (slowly gaining general acceptance) and, to further confuse the issue, a Commitment Grade, also using Roman numerals, currently from I to VII.

Ice grading
Three systems are most frequently used: the Scottish grades (I to VI) in the UK, Alps and New Zealand; the Canadian grades in Canada and the USA, where a Technical Grade of 1 to 8 and a Commitment Grade (see above) are used e.g. VI/WI7+ is a very committing route at grade 7+; or Mixed Grades (M1 to M10) for modern ice routes such as The Empire Strikes Back. In addition, R (risky) or x (fragile) might be added.

Note on metric / imperial measurements in this title
Imperial conversions of metric peak heights (or vice versa) reflect as accurately as possible the original measurement, while conversions of the route lengths of climbs are given as reasonable approximations to the original.

Aid climbing
Aid climbing is rated from A0 ('pulling' on a piece of gear to help you get past a difficult move) to A5 (very dangerous aid climbing, with the potential of a fatal fall).

Mixed routes
Routes that incorporate rock climbing as well as aid, ice and snow, and other objective difficulties are rated in a multiple fashion, e.g. a grade of VI/5.11/A4/WI5+ might be given to a route on Cerro Torre, Patagonia. Here VI stands for Commitment or Alpine Grade VI; 5.11 for free rock climbing on the USA scale; A4 for aid; and WI5+ as the Technical Ice Grade (degrees 1 to 8). The combination of the grades tells climbers that this is a very serious route indeed!

In some cases (e.g. Eternal Flame on the Trango Towers), the opening party gave a grade of IX- (UIAA) with a comparative USA grade in brackets (5.12c) to avoid confusion with the Alpine scale (I to VII).

Right American climbing legend Lynn Hill breezing up the formidably overhanging second (crux) pitch, Serpentine, Taipan Wall, Australia.

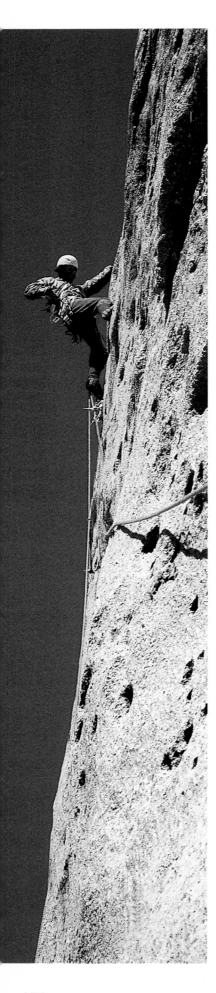

Left Czechoslovakian Igor Koller leading the sparsely protected 18th pitch on a new variation to Weg durch den Fisch, Italian Dolomites.

Right Briton Stevie Haston opening the mixed route Welcome to the Machine, in Val Vasavarenche, Italy; it was the first M9 in the world.